REVELATION

READING AND INTERPRETING THE BIBLE SERIES

REVELATION

DAN BOONE

Copyright © 2022 by Dan Boone

The Foundry Publishing®
PO Box 419527
Kansas City, MO 64141
thefoundrypublishing.com

ISBN 978-0-8341-4057-8

Printed in the
United States of America

All rights reserved. No part of this publication may be reproduced, stored in a retrieval system, or transmitted in any form or by any means—for example, electronic, photocopy, recording—without the prior written permission of the publisher. The only exception is brief quotations in printed reviews.

Cover design: Caines Design
Interior design: Jody Langley

Unless otherwise indicated, all Scripture quotations are from the New Revised Standard Version Bible (NRSV), copyright © 1989 National Council of the Churches of Christ in the United States of America. All rights reserved worldwide.

The following copyrighted version of Scripture is used by permission:
The Holy Bible, New International Version® (NIV®). Copyright © 1973, 1978, 1984, 2011 by Biblica, Inc.™ Used by permission of Zondervan. All rights reserved worldwide. www.zondervan.com. The "NIV" and "New International Version" are trademarks registered in the United States Patent and Trademark Office by Biblica, Inc.™

Library of Congress Cataloging-in-Publication Data
A complete catalog record for this book is available from the Library of Congress.

The internet addresses, email addresses, and phone numbers in this book are accurate at the time of publication. They are provided as a resource. The Foundry Publishing® does not endorse them or vouch for their content or permanence.

10 9 8 7 6 5 4 3 2 1

Contents

Introduction 7

1. The Revelation: Apocalypse, Prophecy, and Epistle 13

2. Revelation: The Plot 41

3. The Entrance 51

4. The Bad News and the Good News 75

5. The Response of the People 163

6. Blessing-Benediction 183

Bibliography 189

Introduction

Who can see into the future? In 1932, Aldous Huxley published *A Brave New World*. This remarkable book has fascinated us for almost a century with its uncanny look into the days in which we are now living. His book

> predicted and portrayed a seemingly fantastic future: a world of globalization, runaway commercialism, genetic engineering, readily available birth control, private helicopters, widespread recreational drug use, mass use of antidepressants, commercial space travel, virtual reality entertainment, hero worship of technologists, the eroticization of children, nearly complete disinterest in history and literature, and deep distraction. It was a world very different from his own, but with many similarities to ours. And it was a warning: that the distractions, pleasures, and technological advances we love could potentially infringe our freedom and distract our humanity.[1]

Is this what the book of Revelation is doing? Do we read this last book of Holy Scripture looking for those foreseen things that are coming true before our very eyes? Are we opening a time capsule buried centuries ago but recently unearthed? Have we, like Nicolas Cage and

---

1. Cherie Harder, introduction to *Selections from a Brave New World*, Trinity Forum Readings (The Trinity Forum, 2018), 3, https://www.ttf.org/product/brave-new-world/.

his friends in the movie *National Treasure*, followed the hidden clues to treasures we never imagined? Are we in the middle of a mysterious Agatha Christie novel or a Sherlock Holmes saga? Are we solving mathematical riddles and complex puzzles? Yes and no.

Yes, we are reading a book about what is happening in our world today, a world where humans are distracted by the dazzling powers that intend to rule us. Yes, there are clues that we need to pay attention to. There are things to figure out. Yes, it is a book that is laced with warnings about the world we are experiencing and the dangers that lurk where dark powers have their way. Yes, it is about the future of humanity.

But also, no. It is not a riddle to be mastered, a crime to be sleuthed, or a math problem to be solved. The book of Revelation is not meant to be deciphered or figured out. It is not a connect-the-dots puzzle between the predictions of the first century and the characters and events of our century. If the opening verses carry any weight, it is a book meant to be read aloud and heard. "Blessed is the one who reads aloud the words of the prophecy, and blessed are those who hear and who keep what is written in it" (1:3). There is nothing here about solving riddles, predicting futures, or finding buried treasure—but there are sightings of a brave new world.

We have a hard time reading the Revelation rightly because we are accustomed to reading it as we do the rest of the Bible. Read Mark's account of Jesus and then go to Revelation 1:12-13, where on the island of Patmos the same Jesus stands in the midst of the seven golden lampstands; it feels as if we've been transported to a different planet. And in literary terms, we have been. It is the equivalent of reading David McCullough's book *1776*, on the American Revolution, one minute, and turning the page to find the Marvel Avengers and X-Men waiting for us the next. We go from Herod, the Pharisees, and blind Bartimaeus to red dragons, horsemen of the Apocalypse, and prostitutes riding sidesaddle on the back of sea monsters. We know one of these worlds. We feel lost in the other—until we learn to read the Revelation with a new set of eyes.

The way we learned to read has done us no favors. We hold a book in our hands and look down on it. Our hands control the book. The book needs our right and left hand beneath it to leverage its weight. Or we carefully cock our thumb in the spine of the book with the other four supporting fingers holding it aloft. The book cannot stand on its own. It needs us to hold it up. And we hold it where we wish. We position it the right distance from our eyes to allow our eyes to see what we want. We can tilt it to allow light to reflect off its pages. As we read, the book is beneath our gaze. We hover in power over it, deciding which parts to read and which to skip, which to peruse slowly and which to skim, which to underline and which to ignore. We can do with the text what we please. If we are students, we will seek to master what we read so that we can spit it back out on the upcoming test that determines our grade. We want to master the text, conquer it, and be ready to explain it in our own words. In the assigned book reports we write, we summarize the book and make statements about what it intended, about its strengths and weaknesses. We judge the book. This is how we learned to read.

We as a world are like this—dismantling things, tearing them down to their individual parts, and then putting them back together again for our purposes. We have done this with the elements of the periodic table, the atom, the gene, digital sound, and even companies. We have the power to tear a company apart, sell its pieces, and keep what we wish. We can take oxygen, nitrogen, and potassium and make things. And we do. We can also assemble odd pieces from the dictionary to make our own meaning. We build worlds out of the words we choose to use. And when we read the Bible, all of this comes into play.

Reading is about power. I believe that this is the reason behind all the bizarre interpretations of the book of Revelation. We don't know what else to do with the book except power up and conquer it. For this reason, we have deciphered its numbers, named its modern antichrists, assigned its Armageddon opponents, and declared the identity of its beasts. We have corralled it into our timetable and calendared its conclusion. We have mastered the book because that is how we read. We take power over words and create our own realities.

But what if the book has breath in it, breath other than our own? What if the book is not an inanimate object to be controlled by our hands, eyes, and judgments? What if there is another power at work in the act of reading? What if we are being held in hands, discerned through eyes, and judged by divine insight? What if this book places us under the examination of one who sees deeply into us and knows us? What if this examining Spirit is acting on us? What if *we* are *being* read? Well, that's a whole different way of reading the Revelation—or being read by it.

Our reading is also impacted by our situation in life. Personally, I can only read the Revelation as a privileged person—privileged by gender, race, education, wealth, and nationality. I cannot read the Revelation as a poor woman in a nation under terrorist rule. I cannot read it as a single mother of two who struggles to make ends meet on government support. I cannot read it as an immigrant, a black man, an illiterate coal miner, or a sex-trafficking slave.

The Revelation seems to be one of those books that are best read from a position of no power. People of privileged power do not know what else to do with the book, so they master it for end-time thrillers and attention-getting prophecies. The very beasts that the Revelation reveals protect many of the privileges that people with power enjoy. The more we are invested in these beastly power systems, the less we want them toppled by a slaughtered lamb. We do not have the eyes to see that dark powers have their hooks deep into our privileged lives. So we read the Revelation for futuristic speculation rather than immediate repentance. Nevertheless, the warnings in the book are aimed directly at folk like us. We are being exposed so that we might be saved.

People without power tend to find the book easier to read. They know what it is like to have destructive horses ride through their lives wreaking havoc. They have seen a dragon with seven heads vomit a flood in their direction. They remember the "dis-ordered" nights when the stars seemed to fall out of the sky and pepper the world with chaos. They are not strangers to the book in the same way the privileged are. When they read it, joy rises in their hearts when the beast finally gets what's coming to him and when they, who had no hope, get more than they ever imagined from the one who sits on a throne.

Aldous Huxley imagined a brave new world. So does the Revelation. Both rise from a real history in time and yet seem to supersede that time to say things that are important to all humans. Both are imaginative. Both are free from the constraints of scenes and characters of the world here and now. They are free to name the culprits and paint them liberally. And they are free to make unsuspecting heroes of simple people. The Revelation evokes a new world whose seeds are planted in the heart of every human longing.

1

The Revelation: Apocalypse, Prophecy, and Epistle

Three very different literary genres combine to give the Revelation its uniqueness. All are found throughout Scripture, but we are more familiar with prophecy and epistles than we are with apocalyptic literature.

Apocalyptic Literature

Apocalyptic literature is an ancient genre classification. It consists of visions and revelations to human recipients by otherworldly beings. Two opposing worlds are colliding. The content has a narrative spine, but its plot is beyond the scope of history as a reference point. In addition, its images and characters are larger than life. The repeated phrase "and then I saw . . ." is the portal from one vision to another. In the Revelation, we visit six or seven stories, all about the same thing but told in differing ways. The dragon is in some stories but not in others. The one who sits on the throne is dominant in some stories but absent in others.

The Revelation is handed off four times. It comes to John by way of God, who entrusts the message to the exalted Son of Man-Messiah, who gives it to an angel, who gives it to John with the command that he write down what he has seen and deliver it to the seven churches. The seven churches each have an angel, a corporate spirit that represents the church's essence and serves as the persona of the church. God addresses the letters to the angels of the churches. While the transmission of the Revelation is shrouded in mystery and dependent on heavenly beings, it finds its way into human hands by the obedience of a man named John, exiled like many of his forerunners of faith.

The Revelation, though written as a narrative, is not told in a sequential start-to-finish order. It revisits the same truths in narrative form from differing perspectives. While there is some progress from suffering to victory, the path is not straightforward. The Revelation is like a tornado moving across land. While the path of the tornado may be from one point to another, the direction of the wind is circular. It repeats the same circle numerous times, picking up speed and leaving affected readers in its wake—until it moves ahead toward a climactic end. We see the same power repeated in multiple scenes. We become familiar with a trail of judgment and destruction as fractions of creation are affected with each spin of the wind.

> **The Revelation is like a tornado moving across land. While the path of the tornado may be from one point to another, the direction of the wind is circular.**

Apocalyptic is still among us. It is a very current way of expressing truth. Current movie examples are *The Hunger Games*, *The Matrix*, and *Star Wars*. These stories have connections to realities that we know, but the characters are larger than life, sometimes otherworldly, and quite fantastic.

The Revelation: Apocalypse, Prophecy, and Epistle

The 1999 film *The Matrix*, starring Keanu Reeves, is a work of science fiction. It envisions a world in which humans experience a false reality known as the Matrix, which was constructed by their captors—machines capable of advanced intelligence. The Matrix was designed to maintain control over the humans, whose bodies were actually serving as living batteries for their machine overlords. Neo, the Keanu Reeves character, awakens to this reality, along with several other humans. Together these freed humans rebel against the machines. Interestingly, *The Matrix* and its sequels "inspired books and theories expanding on . . . religious and philosophical ideas alluded to in the films."[1]

A similar apocalyptic movie is *The Hunger Games*, based on the 2008 novel of the same title by Suzanne Collins. In the novel, set in the future, Katniss Everdeen, aged sixteen,

> lives in the . . . post-apocalyptic nation of Panem in North America. The Capitol, a highly advanced metropolis, exercises political control over the rest of the nation. The Hunger Games is an annual event in which one boy and one girl aged 12-18 from each of the twelve districts surrounding the Capitol are selected by lottery to compete in a televised battle [royal] to the death.
>
> . . . In writing *The Hunger Games*, Collins drew upon Greek mythology, Roman gladiatorial games, and contemporary reality television for thematic content.[2]

If these worlds feel odd and strange to you, welcome to the Revelation. These movies are our apocalyptic literature, comic books, games,

---

1. Wikipedia, s.v. "*The Matrix*," last modified January 25, 2022, 03:41, https://en.wikipedia.org/wiki/The_Matrix.
2. Wikipedia, s.v. "*The Hunger Games* (novel)," last modified January 13, 2022, 11:10, https://en.wikipedia.org/wiki/The_Hunger_Games_(novel).

and stories. They mesh visible and invisible worlds, normality and abnormality, and powers that are otherworldly with characters that live in the world we know.

Apocalyptic literature is not a connect-the-dots mystery to be solved but rather images that work on our imaginations in ways that allow us to back away from the world we live in. We come to understand it better by viewing it at a distance. There is enough resemblance to the historical context to keep us on the planet but enough dissonance from the daily grind to assure us that we are not in Kansas anymore.

Apocalyptic is an imaginative way to tell the story. Eugene Peterson comments, "Everything in the Revelation can be found in the previous sixty-five books of the Bible. The Revelation adds nothing of substance to what we already know. The truth of the gospel is already complete, revealed in Jesus Christ. There is nothing new to say on the subject. But there is a new way to say it. I read the Revelation not to get more information but to revive my imagination."[3]

For three hundred years, apocalyptic literature flourished in the land of the Jews. You find good examples in Daniel, Isaiah 24–27, Zechariah 9–14, Ezekiel 38–39, Matthew 24–25, Mark 13, Luke 21, and 1 Thessalonians 4:16–5:11.

> Apocalyptic literature flourished in Judaism between the third century BC and the second century AD. At least 14 non-canonical Jewish apocalypses were produced during this time. . . . After the two disastrous revolts of the Jews in Palestine against the Romans (AD 66-74 and AD 132-135), both of which were fueled by apocalyptic

---

[3]. Eugene Peterson, *Reversed Thunder: The Revelation of John and the Praying Imagination* (San Francisco: HarperSanFrancisco, 1991), xi.

expectations, apocalyptic literature fell into disrepute within Judaism, but not within Christianity. The book of Revelation is the only full apocalypse in the New Testament. . . . In addition to the book of Revelation, Christian writers produced more than twenty apocalypses in the early centuries of the Christian church.[4] Apocalyptic writings share eight common characteristics:

1. *Dualism.* Like a football game, there are two opposing teams on the field. A line is drawn in the dirt separating the opposing forces: God versus Satan, light versus darkness, the Lamb versus the beast, the coming reign of God versus this present evil age, heaven versus earth, suffering today versus celebration tomorrow.

   The decisive shift from this present evil age with its suffering to the celebrated reign of God is an emphatic move on God's part. In apocalyptic literature, the future does not slowly emerge like a snake crawling out of its skin. It comes like a hawk swooping down on a field mouse. In the Revelation, the activity of God is usually swift and conclusive. God brings life as we know it to a halt, and we become part of a new reality.

2. *Pessimism.* Apocalyptic is written to people who have no power. They are the pawns of social and political empires that spill over into their lives. The historic context that calls apocalyptic into existence is pessimistic: the world is not going in the right direction, and there seems to be nothing we can do about it.

---

[4]. Al Truesdale, "The Genre of the Book of Revelation," A Resource for Clergy of the Tennessee District Church of the Nazarene (2013 Seminar), 3.

Little hope is placed in human solutions. Rather, our hope is in a move from beyond history, where God does something dramatically redeeming.

The biblical writers had seen failed kings, broken covenants, and crushing defeats by pagan armies. They concluded that God could no longer work from within history to accomplish his purposes. Fickle humans could never establish the reign of God. A new future would require an outside-of-history move. While the context that calls for apocalyptic was pessimistic, the outcome of the activity of God was always hope inspiring.

Apocalyptic writings not only offered hope and comfort, they also served as protest literature. They protested the prevailing worldview embodied in the dominant culture. Apocalyptic writers encouraged their readers not to accept the beliefs and lifestyles of the world around them, but . . . to remain faithful to God. Because of the belief that history was in God's hands . . . , apocalyptic writers did not call for social or political action. The transcendent world that had been revealed to them presented clear evidence that in God's ultimate design, evil, pain, suffering, violence, and injustice do not belong and will not have the final word.[5]

3. *Determinism.* Determinism is the idea that God's mind is already made up about how history will unfold. And there is no changing the mind of God. History will fall like prearranged dominoes. The end is known at the beginning, and all that is left is

---

5. Ibid., 5.

for us to fall in line. If this view of history is true of the Revelation, then we can look for a hidden code revealing a future antichrist and the date of Armageddon. This makes sense if God has already lined up the dominoes, you and me included.

However, a deterministic view of history is out of character with God. The prophetic view, which I will describe later, is more in keeping with what we find in the Revelation. While we find a deterministic certainty in the ability of God to bring all things together in Christ, we do not find a fatalism that suggests there is nothing we can do. Rather, we find the people of God called to bear costly witness and to challenge the sovereignty of all dark powers by their worship of the Lamb.

4. *Imagery*. Apocalyptic literature is loaded with images not meant to be taken literally. The images convey a meaning. They represent a reality. Movie producers understand this. Movies such as *I, Robot* and *The Matrix* take us into the future. To say that the images of the Revelation are not meant to be taken literally is not to say that they have no meaning. The book of Revelation does not mean what it says; *it means what it means.* We see beasts rising from pits, seven-headed animals, blood flowing as high as horses' bridles, angels dumping bowls of fire onto the earth, and locusts that sting like scorpions. These graphic images have meaning. But to interpret them literally is to bypass their meaning in favor of limiting the text to

> The book of Revelation does not mean what it says; *it means what it means.*

our interpretation. When our morbid fascination seizes biblical symbols to serve our anxious interests, we violate the meaning intended by the writer. We also eliminate the original readers. In reading the Revelation, we must ask, What did these images mean to those who first heard them? We must allow the book to speak to us in its strangeness rather than tame it with our self-serving interpretation.

Symbols in Revelation carry the book's message; they are not the book's message itself. The two are not to be confused. The symbols are given to help Christians see the world—heaven and earth—as it truly is, and not as the claimant powers of the world want us to see it. . . . The symbols are meant to help us see all things in the light of God's sovereignty as manifest in the person of the crucified and risen Lamb of God.[6]

5. *Numerology.* The Revelation is loaded with numbers. The numbers have meaning beyond their numerical value.
   - 7 = wholeness, completeness
   - 3½ years or 42 months or 1,260 days = incompleteness, usually a time of trial
   - 666 = the name of the beast
   - 12, 24, and 144,000 (multiples of 12) = the people of God

In the Revelation, the reign of persecution and resistance is defined as "a time, and times, and half a time" (Rev. 12:14), which is also 3½ years or 42 months or 1,260 days (v. 6). These four different ways of denoting a given time period are scattered

---
6. Ibid., 6.

throughout the book, calling us to pay attention to what is being said. John uses numbers to make meaning.

The same can be said for colors. White symbolizes righteousness and purity, gold denotes high value, red indicates destruction and bloody death, and purple indicates royalty. The colors of the four horses of Revelation speak for themselves: the white horse of a conqueror, the red horse of human slaughter, the black horse of economic depression and poverty, and the pale-green horse of death and the grave. The Revelation might have greater appeal in the comic book genre, with larger-than-life mythical characters, brilliant colors, and symbolic images. It is more than words on a page; it is theater with all the senses engaged.

6. *Recapitulation.* This means going over the same subject with variations. The Revelation revisits the same theme about six times. It is similar to a tornado because it moves in a given direction but repeats its spiral multiple times. It is like a miniature racetrack inside a semitruck on a trip from Kansas City to Denver. While the miniature cars are circling the track toward a finish line, the truck is moving toward its destination. Unless readers understand this, they mistake the Revelation for a time line. They try to put things in sequential order, locate where they are on the time line, and predict what is coming down the road. This is not how the Revelation is to be read. It is a tornado that connects heaven and earth, spins in a single narrative unit in

one place, and then moves forward to the next location, carrying with it the images and symbols picked up in previous stories.

7. *Suffering*. Apocalyptic literature is written when things are going bad. You won't find it under David's reign or when God's people are in power. It is the cry from the bottom of the pile. It is the speech of pain. It takes overwhelming catastrophe and hopelessness to birth apocalyptic literature. Suffering birthed the Revelation.

8. *Pseudonymous*. In most apocalyptic literature, the author writes under another name, usually someone of notoriety who lived much earlier. Religious apocalyptic titles include *The Life of Adam and Eve* and *The Apocalypse of Moses*. Why would writers do this? Let's say I am writing in 2019 but I want you to believe my predictions about the year 1999, so I write under the name of John F. Kennedy. My book begins in the 1960s. As you read my apocalypse, you are amazed at my accuracy in predicting the 1970s, 1980s, and 1990s. It's easy to prophesy the past! The further you read, the more convinced you are that I am right about the future.

The Revelation does not demonstrate pseudonymous authorship. John is clearly identified as a pastoral and prophetic figure who is familiar with the historic seven churches.

Prophetic Literature

Three verses into the biblical story, the text reads, "And God said . . ." (Gen. 1:3, NIV). At each paragraph of the creation account, these words are repeated (vv. 3, 6, 9, 14, 20, 24, 26). Every creative move begins with God speaking. The biblical story ends in the closing words of the Revelation with God still speaking: "Surely I am coming soon" (Rev. 22:20). The middle of our story is full of the same: the Lord said to Abraham, the Lord called to Moses from the bush, the Lord spoke to David, and so on.

God speaks. And when God speaks, a prophet is created. Amos writes, "Surely the Lord GOD does nothing, without revealing his secret to his servants the prophets. The lion has roared; who will not fear? The Lord GOD has spoken; who can but prophesy?" (Amos 3:7-8). A prophet is an inspired messenger from God who speaks on behalf of God from an experience with God. John's visionary encounter with the one "like a son of man" (NIV) in Revelation 1:13 is reminiscent of the divine encounter with Jeremiah:

Now the word of the LORD came to me saying,

> "Before I formed you in the womb I knew you,
>
> and before you were born I consecrated you;
>
> I appointed you a prophet to the nations."

Then I said, "Ah, Lord GOD! Truly I do not know how to speak, for I am only a boy." But the LORD said to me,

> "Do not say, 'I am only a boy';
>
> for you shall go to all to whom I send you,
>
> and you shall speak whatever I command you,
>
> Do not be afraid of them,
>
> for I am with you to deliver you,
>
> says the LORD."

Then the Lord put out his hand and touched my mouth; and the Lord said to me,

"Now I have put my words in your mouth." (Jer. 1:4-9)

Encounters with the holy God produced prophets who were compelled to write and speak what they had seen and heard. Prophetic literature is characterized by oracles of salvation and judgment, announcements of coming salvation, the call to repentance, and an injection of hope in the context of despair. In the opening of the Revelation, John writes, "Blessed is the one who reads aloud the words of the prophecy" (1:3).

The Revelation has a variety of prophets, true and false. We meet John the true prophet in the opening chapter of the book. He is "in the spirit on the Lord's day" (v. 10), and he sees a vision of the exalted Son of Man. The encounter is so electrified with holiness that he believes he will die. But Christ places his right hand on John, the hand of blessing, and instructs John: "Do not be afraid; I am the first and the last, and the living one. I was dead, and see, I am alive forever and ever; and I have the keys of Death and of Hades. Now write what you have seen, what is, and what is to take place after this" (vv. 17-19). Thus begins the Revelation. It is important to understand this mix of apocalyptic imagery and prophetic urgency. John's encounter with the risen Christ is the occasion in which he receives the Revelation. He stands among the prophets as one who has encountered the holiness of God and lived to tell of it.

We meet other faithful prophets in the Revelation: "And I will grant my two witnesses authority to prophesy for one thousand two hundred sixty days, wearing sackcloth" (11:3). Theirs is a message of repentance, much like the brokenhearted Jeremiah warning the very people who could not see what was obvious to God.

We also meet false prophets in the Revelation. Some are embedded in the seven churches: "You have tested those who claim to be apostles but are not, and have found them to be false" (2:2). "You have some there who hold to the teaching of Balaam" (v. 14). "I have this against you: you tolerate that woman Jezebel, who calls herself a prophet and is teaching and beguiling my servants to practice fornication and to eat food sacrificed to idols" (v. 20).

In Revelation 13:11-18, the second beast performs prophetic functions on behalf of the first beast, the monster of chaos from the sea. In Revelation 16:13, the second beast is called a false prophet: "And I saw three foul spirits like frogs coming from the mouth of the dragon, from the mouth of the beast, and from the mouth of the false prophet." This saga continues in 19:20: "And the beast was captured, and with it the false prophet who had performed in its presence the signs by which he deceived those who had received the mark of the beast and those who worshiped its image."

Whether true or false, prophetic characters function in the Revelation as central players in the cosmic battle. They are the mouthpieces of good and evil.

Prophetic literature has six distinguishing characteristics:

1. *God as Creator.* The prophets connected the God of the beginning with the God of the ending because God cares about creation and intends to redeem it, not destroy it. God will not abandon creation but will bring it to completion. The God we

see in the Revelation is a God who makes all things new, who finishes what was started. As Isaiah spoke of God as Creator in Isaiah 40–55, we find the whole creation, specifically the elements of nature, under the control of a sovereign God in the Revelation.

2. *God as Covenant Maker.* This is where prophetic literature differs a bit from apocalyptic literature. The prophets knew that the disobedience of the covenant people was a large part of the problem. If the people would repent and turn from their wicked ways, God would move to save them. The prophet viewed the saving activity of God and the obedience of the covenant people as symmetrical. Prophetic literature is most often about the sin of the people.

   In some of the letters to the churches (Rev. 2–3), sinful behavior is the topic of concern. However, this behavior is not the heart of the concern. As in most apocalyptic literature, the issue is the greater darkness, the looming empire, or the suffering of saints under beastly powers.

   In addressing these powers, the prophetic voice is optimistic, even in the darkest days. Through a lineage of failed kings and rulers, God will bring forth the Messiah. From the leftovers of exile, God will raise up a righteous remnant. Where apocalyptic was somewhat pessimistic about the power of the people to accomplish God's future, the prophets were radically optimistic. Salvation need not come swooping down from the outside; it arrives as God becomes flesh and blood. God works from within history and humanity. We are partners with God in our redemption.

Apocalyptic literature is like a World Wrestling Entertainment match. Before the two wrestlers crawl in the ring, the outcome is already decided. We just have to wait until the end of the match to know who wins. An apocalyptic view of history is deterministic—God's mind is made up. History is already plotted from beginning to end.

Prophetic literature is like the World Series. The outcome is up for grabs. How each person plays makes a difference in the outcome. It really matters what we do. Prophetic literature calls for ethical responsibility, holy living, repentance from sin, and social justice. The outcome of history is not in the hands of a boxed-in God. The future belongs to a God who makes covenants with people and is free to respond to what we do. God is free to come in mercy or judgment. God is free to bring this present evil age to an end, now or later.

> While there are significant differences between prophetic literature and apocalyptic literature, they find a strange friendship in the Revelation as traits of each make their appearance.

While there are significant differences between prophetic literature and apocalyptic literature, they find a strange friendship in the Revelation as traits of each make their appearance. Overall, it is much more apocalyptic than it is prophetic, but key themes of the prophets make strong appearances: remembering, repentance, avoiding idol sacrifices, faithful witness, and true worship. The Revelation speaks directly to the people of God about their mission in the world—witness and worship—but it does not hinge the hope of victory on the work of the people.

3. *A New Israel and a People of God.* The prophets celebrated God's resolve to create and to preserve a people who worship in spirit and truth. This people, though exiled in response to their sin, are still the people written on God's heart. Their tears are stored in God's bottle. The preservation of a remnant of the faithful is the primary plot of the biblical story. The song of Mary, the Magnificat of Luke 1:46-55, could well be the summation of the apocalyptic message of the Revelation:

> And Mary said,
>> "My soul magnifies the Lord,
>>> and my spirit rejoices in God my Savior,
>> for he has looked with favor on the lowliness of his servant.
>>> Surely, from now on all generations will call me blessed;
>> for the Mighty One has done great things for me,
>>> and holy is his name.
>> His mercy is for those who fear him
>>> from generation to generation.
>> He has shown strength with his arm;
>>> he has scattered the proud in the thoughts of their hearts.
>> He has brought down the powerful from their thrones,
>>> and lifted up the lowly;

> he has filled the hungry with good things,
>> and sent the rich away empty.
> He has helped his servant Israel,
>> in remembrance of his mercy,
> according to the promise he made to our ancestors,
>> to Abraham and to his descendants forever."

The Revelation, while not calling on the promises made to Abraham, is just as concerned with getting a suffering people from their present situation to a future fulfillment. The closing chapters find the prophetic announcement of God:

> See, the home of God is among mortals.
> He will dwell with them as their God;
> they will be his peoples,
> and God himself will be with them;
> he will wipe every tear from their eyes.
> Death will be no more;
> mourning and crying and pain will be no more,
> for the first things have passed away.
> . . . See, I am making all things new. (Rev. 21:3-5)

And if this is not prophetic enough, Jesus speaks in 22:16: "It is I, Jesus, who sent my angel to you with this testimony for the churches. I am the root and the descendant of David." And then in the following verses this warning:

> I warn everyone who hears the words of the prophecy of this book: if anyone adds to them, God will add to that person the plagues described in this book; if anyone takes away from the words of the book of this prophecy, God

will take away that person's share in the tree of life and in the holy city, which are described in this book. (Vv. 18-19)

The meshing of apocalyptic warnings and prophetic language is part of what gives the Revelation its uniqueness among the books of the Bible. The prophetic concern for the preservation of the people of God is as real in the Revelation as in any of the exilic prophets, only stated in a different way.

4. *An Ideal King and Messiah.* At the heart of the prophets was the belief that God would establish a ruler to lead his people. This messianic ruler would rise from the stump of Jesse and shoot up from the root of David. He would be righteous and holy; he would rule with an iron rod. The nations of the world would stream to his holy mountain. The Spirit of the Lord would rest on him in wisdom and power. He would turn swords into plowshares and spears into pruning hooks. This is the anointed one spoken of by the prophets.

We find a similar ruler in the Revelation, but his titles are much more akin to the titles used to depict the emperors of Rome. There are more titles for divinity in the Revelation than there are in any other book. While the central figure is the slaughtered Lamb, who is a prophetic image of the Suffering Servant of God, there are other titles:

- "The Alpha and the Omega" (1:8; 21:6; 22:13)
- "The beginning and the end" (21:6; 22:13)
- "The first and the last" (1:17; 2:8; 22:13)
- "The living one" (1:18)

The Revelation: Apocalypse, Prophecy, and Epistle

- The seven spirits before the throne (1:4; 3:1; 4:5; 5:6)
- "The Amen" (3:14)
- The rider of the white horse (6:2; 19:11)
- The one who makes all things new (21:5)
- "The firstborn of the dead" (1:5)
- The faithful witness (3:14)
- "The ruler of the kings of the earth" (1:5)
- The one "who is and who was and who is to come" (1:4, 8; 4:8)
- "The bright morning star" (22:16)
- The bridegroom (19:7; 21:2, 9)
- The one who is "coming soon" (3:11; 22:7, 12, 20)

All the hopes of humankind are wrapped up in this historical person who is described with a kaleidoscope of images.

5. *A Rebuilt Temple.* The prophets looked forward to a return from Israel and a rebuilding of the Jerusalem temple. This is the one feature of prophetic literature that is rarely found in the Revelation. Luke writes, "The Most High does not dwell in houses made with human hands" (Acts 7:48). As the Revelation describes the new Jerusalem, it notes, "I saw no temple in the city, for its temple is the Lord God the Almighty and the Lamb" (Rev. 21:22).

The Revelation does mention the ark of the covenant. "Then God's temple in heaven was opened, and the ark of his covenant was seen within his temple; and there were flashes of lightning, rumblings, peals of thunder, an earthquake, and heavy hail"

(11:19). The description of the throne of God in Revelation 4–5 has elements of temple language, but it is depicted as a heavenly throne rather than an earthly temple.

Many predictive models of eschatology suggest a literal rebuilding of the Old Testament Jerusalem temple as a sign of the end times. We find no such interest in the Revelation. If anything, we find a clear message that God is interested in a much larger dwelling, a city into which all the nations can bring their labor as an act of worship. It has much more to do with commerce, cultural diversity, and healing for humanity than with animal sacrifice. God's presence will not be limited to tabernacles or temples but will permeate the new heaven and the new earth. The vision of the Revelation is the fulfillment of the intent of the temple—the dwelling of God among the people of God.

6. *The End of Evil.* The prophets imagined a day when evil would no longer exist. It will be destroyed. Lambs will lie down with lions. Cows will graze with bears. Soldiers will turn their weapons into farming tools. While the apocalyptic writers looked for the end of history, the prophets looked for the end of evil within history. The Revelation looks toward the end of evil more than the end of history.

Epistolary Literature

Before summarizing, it is wise to mention that there is another biblical genre found in the Revelation. Epistles were a common form of communication between the apostles and their various congregations. The letters addressed to specific churches included greetings, specific issues of concern, directives, and salutations. These letters were intended for oral delivery to the congregation. The apostolic greeting is found in the opening verses of the Revelation (1:1-8). Blessing is offered to "the one who reads aloud the words of the prophecy" and to "those who hear and who keep what is written in it" (v. 3).

The seven letters of Revelation (chs. 2–3) have many of these same features. One difference we find between the New Testament Epistles of Colossians, Philippians, and Galatians and the letters to the seven churches of the Revelation is that the seven letters are meant to be read to all of the congregations. The "church" being addressed is not just one of the seven churches but all of them, with their different issues. What the Spirit said to one congregation was to be overheard by all.

It is amazing to comprehend that the risen Jesus writes letters to churches—specific churches, troubled and commendable churches. For many, the word "church" does not evoke feelings of deep commitment or devotion. As we often treat grocery stores and telephone companies, we will switch churches in a flash for a better deal. But Jesus cares enough to write letters via John to real congregations in Asia Minor. Neither Jesus nor John could forget the church. The letters appear in geographical order of delivery, following the Roman postal system: Ephesus to Smyrna to Pergamum to Thyatira to Sardis to Philadelphia to Laodicea. John's heart and mind traveled the road his feet knew well.

Each of the seven letters to the seven churches begins with the words "to the angel of the church in [fill in the blank with name of the city] write . . ." Who are these angels? Are they God's "secret service squad" protecting the churches? Are they the UPS delivery system getting the letters from Patmos to the front doors of the seven churches? Are they the pastors of the churches, the messengers of good news (Greek, *angelos*, meaning "messenger")? Who or what is being addressed in the beginning of these letters?

Scott Daniels answers the question in this way:

It is my conviction that John the Revelator writes to the angels of the churches because he recognizes something profound and complex about the way churches are formed as communities. The seven churches of Asia—like all communal bodies—are more than the sum of individuals that make up that community. Communities, like the individual persons from which they are formed, take on a kind of spirit, personality, or "life of their own" that becomes greater than the sum of their individual parts. The seven angels of the seven churches, to whom John writes, are neither disconnected spiritual beings nor a colorful way of describing nonexistent realities. Instead, the term "angel" signifies a very real ethos or communal essence that either gives life to or works at destroying the spiritual fabric of the very community that gave birth to it.[7]

The letters speak to the heart of the church, its essence and character and culture. The church is being exegeted by Christ. Could it be that only Christ can name and address the "angel" of each congregation? Each church is asked to take a listening posture before the one who alone can say, "I know your works, your affliction, your poverty, your city, your challenges."

---

7. T. Scott Daniels, *Seven Deadly Spirits: The Message of Revelation's Letters for Today's Church* (Grand Rapids: Baker Academic, 2009), 17.

Once the angel of each church is summoned, John introduces Jesus to the church. In an epistolary world, titles came at the beginning of the letter. Jesus had plenty:

- The one "who holds the seven stars in his right hand" (Rev. 2:1)
- The one "who walks among the seven golden lampstands" (v. 1)
- "The first and the last" (v. 8)
- The one "who was dead and came to life" (v. 8)
- The one with "the sharp two-edged sword" (v. 12)
- The one with flaming eyes (v. 18)
- The one with burnished-bronze feet (v. 18)
- The one "who has the seven spirits of God" (3:1)
- "The holy one, the true one" (v. 7)
- The one "who opens and no one will shut" (v. 7)
- The one "who shuts and no one opens" (v. 7)
- "The faithful and true witness" (v. 14)
- "The origin of God's creation" (v. 14)

The church is the people who listen to what the Spirit says. While the opening and closing of each letter is similar, the body of each of the letters differs. We find a mixture of affirmation, rebuke, tender encouragement, and phenomenal promises. Jesus gives each church what it needs. He knows where we are, and he wants us to listen. Most of the promises at the end of the letters are drawn from the imagery of the new Jerusalem, the holy city come down in Revelation 21–22. We will move through several stories in chapters 4–20, but the very things God promises the churches will appear again: "the tree of life" (2:7); the abolishment of "the second death" (v. 11); "the hidden manna" (v. 17);

"a white stone" with "a new name" written on it (v. 17); "the morning star" (v. 28); "white robes," names recorded in "the book of life" (3:5); and a dwelling in the city of God (v. 12).

Once we leave the seven letters, we are ushered before the throne of God in Revelation 4. This un-epistle-like imagery is foreign to the apostolic letters. We never return to the epistolary genre until the closing lines of the book. "The one who testifies to these things says, 'Surely I am coming soon.' Amen. Come, Lord Jesus! The grace of the Lord Jesus be with all the saints. Amen" (22:20-21). Revelation opens and closes like a letter from an apostle, uses prophetic authority and language, but allows apocalyptic imagery to carry the weight of the message.

> Revelation opens and closes like a letter from an apostle, uses prophetic authority and language, but allows apocalyptic imagery to carry the weight of the message.

The Revelation: An Apocalypse, a Prophecy, *and* an Epistle

Given this brief introduction to the literary types found in the Revelation, I suggest you read it for yourself. The mistake of many preachers and interpreters is to focus on the small pieces and miss the whole. Read the entire book from start to finish in one sitting. No doubt this is how the people of God received it. They heard the entire letter-prophecy-apocalypse read from beginning to end. It was not consumed as a chapter-by-chapter Bible study. Nor did they pause to try to figure out what each character and image meant. They received it as a whole.

In the words of Eugene Boring,

> # The Revelation: Apocalypse, Prophecy, and Epistle

The last "book" of the Bible is a pastoral letter to Christians in Asia in the late first century who were confronted with a critical religio-political situation, from a Christian prophet who wrote in apocalyptic language and imagery. Like the Bible in general, there is some difficulty in understanding Revelation, but it can and should be understood, for it has had enormous influence on religion, history, and culture and has an urgently needed message for the contemporary church.[8]

Do not be sidetracked by wild speculations about the Revelation. Theories abound. Predictions have taken shape in end-time charts and popular novels. Clever authors have captivated readers with scenarios that focus on the end of time, the annihilation of the earth, Armageddon's bloody battle, rebuilt temples, the mark of the beast, and the beastly Antichrist. An old French proverb says, "Better a terrifying end, than this endless terror." It seems as if many prefer believing in predictions of a disastrous end of the world to trusting God for the unknown future of our redemption. While these may be interesting speculations, they are well off the beaten path of God's redemption of all things.

When we take authority over the text to tinker with its various pieces, we fail to hear what the Spirit is saying to the church. We find ourselves playing connect the dots between textual images and current personalities and events. This can absorb us in speculation. The moment the Revelation becomes a source book for prognosticating or a document to be deciphered, it loses its breath. It becomes dead words

---

[8]. M. Eugene Boring, *Revelation*, Interpretation: A Bible Commentary for Teaching and Preaching (Louisville, KY: John Knox Press, 1989), 1.

on a page. The God-breathed Scriptures are more than this. As we read the Revelation, the Spirit is at work forming us as a holy people.

In Herman Melville's novel *White Jacket* one of the sailors takes sick with severe stomach pains. Dr. Cuticle, the ship's surgeon, is delighted to have a patient with something more challenging to his art than blisters. He diagnoses appendicitis. Several shipmates are impressed into nursing service. The deckhand is laid out on the operating table and prepared for surgery. Dr. Cuticle goes at his work with verve and skill. He makes his cuts with precision, and, on the way to excising the diseased organ, points out interesting anatomical details to the attendants around the table, who had never before seen the interior of an abdomen. He is absorbed in his work, and obviously good at it. All in all, it is an impressive performance, but the sailor attendants are, to a man, not impressed but appalled. The poor patient, by the time he has been sewn up, has been a long time dead on the table. Dr. Cuticle, enthusiastic in his surgery, hadn't noticed. The sailors, shy in their subservience, didn't tell him.[9]

All too easily, what began as living breath becomes as dead as a cadaver. We are left to poke, probe, dissect, analyze, and autopsy. And like Dr. Cuticle, many of us were never aware of the moment when the breathing stopped. "All scripture is inspired by God and is useful for teaching, for reproof, for correction, and for training in righteousness, so that everyone who belongs to God may be proficient, equipped for every good work" (2 Tim. 3:16).

---

9. Eugene Peterson, *Working the Angles: The Shape of Pastoral Integrity* (Grand Rapids: Eerdmans, 1987), 107.

We are not free to violate the biblical texts for our interpretative pleasure, nor may we use them as fodder for best-selling end-time novels. To do so is an affront to God. Jürgen Moltmann writes,

> End-time histories might better be referred to as exterminism. These are acts of military, economic, or ecological violence. Anyone who talks about "the apocalypse" or "the battle of Armageddon" is providing a religious interpretation for mass human crime, and is trying to make God responsible for what human beings are doing. Nothing has a more fatal effect than the expectation of a fatal future. These "cosmic catastrophe promoters" do not awaken the faith and hope of people. The only result is a general alarmism. What Christian apocalyptic intends is not to evoke horror in the face of the end, but to encourage endurance in resisting the powers of this world. Anyone who interprets the threatening nuclear annihilation of humanity apocalyptically as Armageddon is pushing onto God the responsibility of human beings. This is the height of godlessness and irresponsibility. This type of apocalyptic must be exposed.[10]

> **Christian apocalyptic prophecy is not about the end of the world. It is about the new beginning that God creates for us.**

Christian apocalyptic prophecy is not about the end of the world. It is about the new beginning that God creates for us. We believe in the God who raises the dead, who makes all things new, who finishes what was started, who is free to love creation and creatures forever.

---

10. Jürgen Moltmann, *The Coming of God: Christian Eschatology*, trans. Margaret Kohl (Minneapolis: Fortress Press, 1996), 203.

This God is not plotting to destroy us. This God is coming from the future to save us. And our role is to bear costly witness while worshipping the Lamb. In doing this, we will endure to the end—which is our beginning.

2

Revelation: The Plot[1]

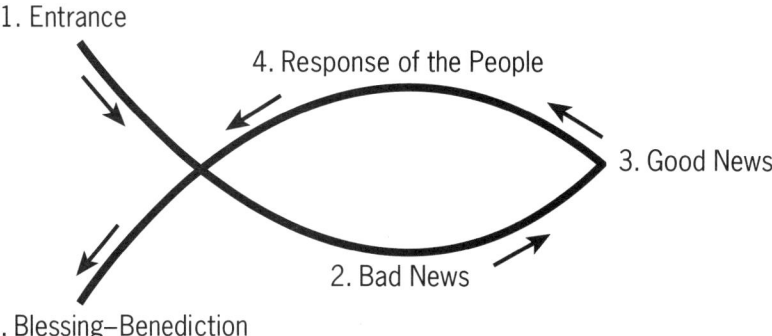

Reading the Revelation of Jesus to John is a lot like reading a comic book or watching an action movie or attending a Broadway theatrical production. You are in the presence of staging, symbolic props, lighting, character development, musical arrangements, colors, texture, volume, imagery, smells, costumes, and crowd reactions. You are attending an event that is happening. The writers, directors, and actors are engaged in creating a particular experience. In many ways, you are unaware of all that is happening subliminally to you as you partake of the experience.

---

1. Concepts and diagrams introduced in this chapter and depicted and discussed throughout this book are adapted and described in greater detail in my earlier book on worship, *The Worship Plot: Finding Unity in Our Common Story* (Kansas City: Beacon Hill Press of Kansas City, 2007).

For example, experience this:

A great portent appeared in heaven: a woman clothed with the sun, with the moon under her feet, and on her head a crown of twelve stars. She was pregnant and was crying out in birth pangs, in the agony of giving birth. Then another portent appeared in heaven: a great red dragon, with seven heads and ten horns, and seven diadems on his heads. His tail swept down a third of the stars of heaven and threw them to the earth. Then the dragon stood before the woman who was about to bear a child, so that he might devour her child as soon as it was born. And she gave birth to a son, a male child, who is to rule all the nations with a rod of iron. But her child was snatched away and taken to God and to his throne; and the woman fled into the wilderness, where she has a place prepared by God, so that there she can be nourished for one thousand two hundred sixty days. (Rev. 12:1-6)

In this short text we have the trappings of theater at its best: a curtain that opens inviting the audience into another world; a character in distress; costumes made of sunbeams; staging in the fly space; the piercing screams of birth pangs; symbols of power in crowns, numbers, and colors; a destructive villain; cataclysmic props falling from the rafters of the universe; a baby born and snatched to safety; clues to the identity of the child from Psalm 2; a scene change to a wilderness; and a reference to a mysterious number of days—1,260. What does all this mean? It means we are in the middle of a story that means something.

In essence, a plot is afoot. We know about literary plots, movie plots, and assassination plots. In all of these, characters are part of a larger story that is about them but also about more than them. Stories have structured moves. The sitcoms that have lasted in syndication follow a beaten path. They open in the normal settings of the worlds they have created—the Central Perk Coffee Shop, Jerry Seinfeld's apartment, the office cubicles of Dunder Mifflin. A story begins by placing us in a familiar world. We are not ready to hear a story until we have located ourselves. Even fairy tales begin by creating a world in which the story can occur: "Once upon a time in a land far away . . ." This move is called the *Entrance*. We are locating ourselves in the presence of specific places, characters, and events.

Before we know it, a hint of trouble appears on the horizon. We don't have a story until one of our characters is in trouble. Stories are about how people encounter the challenges of life. In *Seinfeld*, we see a hint of trouble coming with something that George is doing. Or in *The Office*, Dwight has come up with a risky fire drill to test his colleagues' preparedness. Bad news is on the way. This is the second move of a story—the *Bad News*. It is usually introduced by villains, chaos, or interruptions to the normal flow of life. By the first commercial break, our characters are deep in trouble.

Then comes what we have been waiting for—the heroes who get people out of trouble by saving them, teaching them something, or overcoming the villains. This action is the pinnacle of the story. We can't leave our characters hanging in the balance. Sitcoms and short stories don't work like series shows. They resolve everything in twenty-three minutes plus commercials. Resolution comes in the third move of the sitcom—the *Good News*.

Once the hero or star does the good deed, the characters who have been saved or helped respond. This is where George utters a cry of relief after getting pulled out of his dilemma often by some inadvertent but connected action of Jerry, Kramer, or Elaine—or even by something or someone unexpected. The office workers of Dunder Mifflin respond in relief after Jim—or even Michael—saves them from one of Dwight's misguided schemes. The good news gets into people in ways that cause them to respond. This fourth move is called the *Response of the People*.

The final scene occurs following the last commercial. We return for one brief minute to see the world made right again, normalized, put back on its pedestal. A kingdom from beyond has broken into time and changed it. It is a *Blessing-Benediction* of sorts, a recognition that we can get on with our lives.

Sitcoms follow a pattern: Entrance, Bad News, Good News, Response, and Blessing-Benediction. But this is nothing new to the people of God. This is how the narrative of our Scriptures has worked.

The Creation Story

1. Entrance: the earth was formless and void; God created.
2. Bad News: and the serpent said to the woman . . . , and they hid from God.
3. Good News: God made them clothes . . . ; the seed of the woman will crush the serpent's head.
4. Response of the People: Eve bore children.
5. Blessing-Benediction: life goes on outside Eden.

The Noah Story

1. Entrance: evil filled the earth, but there was one righteous man.
2. Bad News: I will destroy the earth by flood.
3. Good News: but God remembered Noah; the rain stopped.
4. Response of the People: they built an altar and offered sacrifice to God.
5. Blessing-Benediction: a rainbow in the sky; never again.

The Egypt Story

1. Entrance: another Pharaoh arose who knew not Joseph.
2. Bad News: kill the baby boys; increase the brick quota.
3. Good News: Moses stood before the bush; tell Pharaoh to let my people go; miracles and plagues.
4. Response of the People: eat the Passover meal; walk through the sea.
5. Blessing-Benediction: freedom before the mountain of a covenant-making God.

Matthew's Story of Jesus

1. Entrance: genealogy, a holy birth.
2. Bad News: Herod, Pharisees, Romans, a cross.
3. Good News: a resurrection affirms everything he said and did.
4. Response of the People: believe; be healed; witness.
5. Blessing-Benediction: go into all the world and make disciples.

Travelers on the Road to Emmaus (Luke 24)

1. Entrance: crucifixion week in Jerusalem.
2. Bad News: we had hoped that he was the one.
3. Good News: Jesus came and walked alongside.
4. Response of the People: he broke bread and their eyes were opened.
5. Blessing-Benediction: they went immediately to tell the disciples.

The Letter to the Philippians

1. Entrance: Paul sitting in prison.
2. Bad News: death may be coming.
3. Good News: the fellowship of Christ in his suffering; whether I live or die.
4. Response of the People: stop arguing; have the same mind; press toward the goal.
5. Blessing-Benediction: God will supply your need.

Our stories are plotted with a recognizable flow. Stories cohere because they move in these structured ways. The Revelation of Jesus to John does this. But it does it differently than do the Gospels. Revelation is several stories about the same thing. They are stitched together in a patchwork of vignettes that draw from each other and play off each other. If you are looking for one sequential story on a single time line, you will not find it. While there is movement from the beginning to the end, several looped stories are being told.

Some writers have referred to this literary method of looping stories as recapitulation. Images are used, used again, and expanded to make a growing impression of the central message. As observed earlier, a tornado is a helpful word picture for describing this literary method. The tornado goes round and round. Its motion is circular, similar to *Entrance, Bad News, Good News, Response of the People,* and *Blessing-Benediction.* As the tornado picks up speed, it accumulates more and more into the vortex of its power. It lifts everything into a suspension. The tornado has a circular motion but also a geographic path. It touches down and rides the ground for a distance. It spins in place while moving forward at the same time. In the several stories of the Revelation, the same circular motion is occurring but in different places with different trajectories and with different characters—but it moves toward an ending. We do not fully know in each given moment the outcome of those swept into the vortex of power. It is all up in the air awaiting the final gust. Yet as every tornado has a center, an eye of the storm, where peace reigns, the Revelation has the same in the one who sits on the throne. Before God, the stormy sea is as rippleless as glass.

> **Revelation is several stories about the same thing. They are stitched together in a patchwork of vignettes that draw from each other and play off each other.**

Each vision of the Revelation creates a world that we *Enter*—the island of Patmos, the seven churches, the heavenly throne room, earth with rampaging horsemen of the Apocalypse, and so on. The *Bad News* arrives with the introduction of characters such as Jezebel, a red dragon, a beast from the sea, and a prostitute dressed in imperial finery. The *Good News* arrives in the action of characters such as the one who sits on the throne, a slaughtered lamb, the archangel of God, and the faithful witness. The *Response of the People* occurs in songs, sacrifice, and testimony. The *Blessing-Benediction* is in seven beatitudes, a new Jerusalem, and the city come down from heaven.

In reading Revelation, we will examine its worlds and characters, its symbols and numbers and colors. This will help us to read with our eyes open to the experience intended in the writing of this remarkable apocalypse to the church.

If this apocalyptic world feels strange to you, step into the strangeness. I was recently watching my grandson play a video game. There were heroes and villains in cosmic battle. To understand the game, you had to know the powers inherent in each character and select which characters to pit against each other. I felt like a novice. I lost game after game. Finally, my grandson looked at me. "Poppa, I thought maybe you were losing because you are slow with the remote controls. Now I realize that you don't know the story that is happening. You keep getting the good guys and the bad guys mixed up. You can't win at this game unless you know the story."

Our stories tell us who we are. They are the identifying markers of our lives. Deep in the human heart is the desire to know who we are. We want to know to whom we belong and who belongs to us. We want a clear *ought* to inform our choices. We want to know where we have been and where we are going. Lacking this, we wander aimlessly. We fight to secure our place. We compromise to get along. We use or are used. We bow to the idols of promise. We are pawns of those in power. This need not be. We have a story, an old story.

At the heart of our Christian identity is the person of Jesus. His story is gospel because it is the good-news story that makes the world right. It goes like this: And the Spirit came upon Mary, and the child she bore was holy, God's Son. Filled with the Spirit, Jesus became the flesh-and-blood vision statement of God. Every promise in the Law leaped to life in his words and deeds. In him, we saw holiness. His loyalty to the Father was unquestioned; his worship, undivided; his obedience, uncompromised. He treated his brothers and sisters with respect and care. He moved mercifully toward the poor and the outcast. He viewed all creation as a gift, from bread to fish to pungent perfume. "In him was life, and the life was the light of all people" (John 1:4).

Jesus moved among us, liberating us from demons and disease, labels and legalism, death and destruction. Then one dark afternoon, he died in our place. We stood under a blood-smeared post. He took our sin upon himself and went into every dark place we would ever be asked to go, even the pit of death. There he faced down the powers of death, chaos, hell, and the grave. God raised him from the dead, and fifty days later he breathed the Holy Spirit on us.

Holiness is possible because God gives us the Spirit of the risen Christ. We embrace each day as a new creation. We live as the sanctified, free children of God. The promise of God fuels our hope. One day the lamb will lie down with the lion, peace will cover the earth, justice will flow like a mighty stream, and every knee shall bow and every tongue proclaim that Jesus is Lord!

This is our story. In this story, we know who and whose we are. We are the body of Christ, the lampstand of the gospel in a dark world, the church empowered by the Spirit of God. And we are radically optimistic about our future. We embrace tomorrow with faith because God calls us to be a holy people and makes it possible by the Spirit.

This is how the gospel story sounds when Matthew, Mark, Luke, and John tell it. But when we enter the visions of The Revelation, Patmos John tells the story quite differently. It is the same story told apocalyptically. In the pages that follow, we will visit the Revelation from the framework of a story. And in doing so, we will hear the Spirit once again tell us who we are in the middle of worlds where dark powers threaten, where compromise is tempting, and where saints suffer.

3

The Entrance

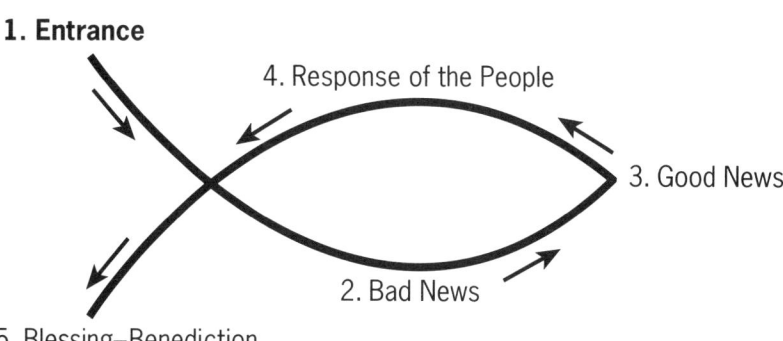

Stories have beginnings that allow readers to locate themselves. Consider the opening "Once upon a time in a land far, far away . . ." Although it is vague, we begin to get a sense of where we are. The *Entrance* is how we know where we are in the story we are about to hear.

At the entrance of a home, a building, or a room, there is usually an indicator of its location: a street sign, an address number, a room name or number, and so on. People looking for a place want to know they have found it. Our *Entrance* to Revelation has several components to it—location in time, location in space, and location in the presence of others. When are we? Where are we? Who are we with? These plot questions must be answered for stories to make sense.

Entrance: Location in Time

We are quickly told that we are in the days following the resurrection of Jesus, during the lifetime of the servant-prophet John, and that the vision we are about to hear occurs on the Lord's Day. It is intentional that we are entering a story that occurs on the Lord's Day, the Christian Sabbath, the first day of the week, the new dawn of resurrection future. While the Old Testament children of God viewed the Sabbath as Saturday, the early church gathered on the first day of the week to celebrate the resurrection, thus our Christian Sabbath. The letters to the churches will be read on the first day of the week. The heavenly scene in Revelation 4 envisions the worship of the saints around the throne as a finished, victorious Sabbath. The time we are to be conscious of is the time of God's great victory.

Christian Sabbath worship is the declaration that God has begun, in the resurrection of Jesus, making all things new. We begin each new block of time, the first day of each new week, by gathering to worship the God who raises the dead. The Sabbath is our entrance into the new week. By gathering in our sanctuaries, we recall *where* we are in time. God tells us *when* we are.

Unlike the ancient Romans, Christians tell time based, not on the story of a Roman emperor, but on the activity of God. In a sense, Christians Christianized the Roman calendar. The lectionary year, the Christian calendar, begins our story, not on New Year's Day, but on the first Sunday of Advent, the season of preparing and waiting for the coming of God in Christ. As the year unfolds, the unique story of God suggests that we are to live our days in faithful witness to God's time. Our calendar says the following:

- Christ appeared in response to the longings of his people.
- Light has entered the dark world in the person of Jesus.
- Suffering is the way of God in the world evidenced by our journey from Ash Wednesday to the cross, the death, and the burial of Jesus.
- Resurrection is God's response to certify the life and ministry of his Son.
- We celebrate the resurrection for seven weeks as we wait for the promised gift of the Holy Spirit to empower us for God's mission in the world.
- We live in ordinary time under the guidance of the Spirit as we bear witness to God.

Our high and holy days are not the same as those celebrated by our culture. We live by a different time zone, though navigating the same time as our neighbors. It is our weekly gathering in corporate worship that reminds us what time it really is in the world.

Entrance: Location in Space

The God who locates us in time also locates us in space. Abraham came to realize the value of holy places. He piled stones in a heap to mark the spot where God spoke to him. As God's family grew, God gave instructions for a tabernacle. A holy place was sanctified in the middle of the camp. When God's family grew larger still, and settled in towns and cities, a temple followed. The Spirit engine of the temple was the holy of holies, the innermost shrine, where the life-giving

Spirit resided. The arrangement of the temple from outer court to inner shrine was designed to remind people of their location in the presence of a holy God.

In the New Testament, we encounter a new understanding of "temple" as Jesus becomes the location of the presence of God in the world. The religious leaders sought to protect the temple by laws that controlled access to God, or so they thought. But God could not be consigned to a location. God is always moving out into the world and refuses to be managed or kept by his creatures. Stephen, in his New Testament martyrdom speech, declares that God will not live in temples "made by human hands" (Acts 7:48, NIV). According to Stephen, God's preferred temple is a people.

The architecture of our buildings can be a wonderful reminder to us that we are God's people. But beautiful architecture alone can never contain God. As we enter the Sunday morning sanctuary, we need to remember that we are a called-together people. God resides in the middle of the gathered church, not in the building. Place is made sacred as God lives among the people who gather there.

In April 2000, I was in Moscow working with Christian leaders. We toured several cathedrals in the Kremlin. As I entered these beautiful churches, my eyes were drawn to the vivid color of the icons and paintings that adorned the rooms. The story of Jesus surrounded me in color, art, and beauty. The Orthodox Church, much better than we Protestants, understands the need to engage the senses in the worship of God. I was sensually engaged in worship as I *read* the story of Christ in the icons. It was a moving experience. As I stood in each cathedral, I felt located. I knew where I was. I was standing in the story of Jesus.

A day later, I worshipped at Moscow First Church of the Nazarene. Fifty to sixty believers gathered on the upper floor of a rented building. The local grocery store was their next-door neighbor in the three-store strip mall. Folding chairs were set up. Portable instruments were brought in. Pulpit furniture was set in place. And we began to worship. A woman testified to the transformation in her life. She graciously thanked a missionary for coming to her city. The missionary then walked all the way to the back of the sanctuary where she stood. He embraced her. The beauty of Christ in that moment rivaled any icon I saw. God does not live in temples made with hands. He lives in the space between people. But these people do gather in temples made by hands.

The staging of the Revelation attends to space in each of the stories that compose the whirl of an apocalyptic tornado.

Revelation 1

We are invited to join John in the Spirit on the Lord's Day. Preaching the word of the Lord and the testimony of Jesus has landed us on exile island, Patmos. Our place in the world is often one of dislocation from the center of power. A dark world prefers that the people of God be off the streets. When our testimony of Jesus complicates the operation of empires, the powers of evil consign us to places out of sight and out of mind. We gather on the fringe of what is going on in the world. Yet it is in these very gatherings that "the ruler of the kings of the earth" appears (1:5). Evicted from positional power, we find ourselves encountered by one who stands in the midst of lampstands (the churches), "clothed with a long robe and with a golden sash across his chest. His head and his hair were white as white wool, white as snow; his eyes were like a flame of fire, his feet were like burnished bronze, refined as in a furnace, and his voice was like the sound of many waters. In his right hand he held seven stars, and from his mouth came a sharp, two-edged sword, and his face was like the sun shining with full force" (vv. 13-16). Our exile island is not lacking the accoutrements of holiness. We are in the middle of what God is doing, not on the fringe of the world's self-absorbed empires. Do we really know where we are when we gather as the people of God?

Revelation 2–3

Can we imagine that the gathering space of those believers transformed as the vision of John is read in each church? The apocalypse they are about to hear begins with them in mind. This is about the gathered people of God, not about a time line for the end of the world. Enough is mentioned in the seven letters to assure us that God knows our physical location: the place where the Nicolaitans are at work (2:6), the place where the synagogue of Satan is located (v. 9), the city where my servant Antipas was killed (v. 13), the town where Jezebel is "beguiling my servants" (v. 20), the place that seems alive but is dead (3:1), the town where the synagogue of Satan has stripped you of power (vv. 8-9), and the city with lukewarm water (v. 16). And all of these places have names: Ephesus, Smyrna, Pergamum, Thyatira, Sardis, Philadelphia, and Laodicea.

We are about to warp into a different place in chapter 4. The tornado will whirl a different story in a different setting. But the Revelation stories yet to be told all begin in the gathering of local congregations. The Revelation is meant first and foremost for them. It is for the gathered people of God, then and now. These stories are happening in our towns, among our heresies, alongside our idols, in the middle of our failures. Let's not allow these visions to become too otherworldly lest we forget the place we live.

Revelation 4–5

"After this I looked, and there in heaven a door stood open!" (4:1). We are transported to a new place, but we are not actually there. We are peeking through an open door into a throne room. We are still standing in our little house churches in our distressed cities, but John invites us to go somewhere with him. He describes the place we are seeing with the artistry of a master painter: a throne and one seated on the throne who "looks like jasper and carnelian" (v. 3); an emerald rainbow (v. 3); twenty-four little thrones (v. 4); elders dressed in white robes with golden crowns (v. 4); lightning, rumblings, peals of thunder (v. 5); seven flaming torches (v. 5); a sea of glass (v. 6); four living creatures with eyes in front and back (v. 6); a lion, an ox, a human, an eagle (v. 7); six wings on each creature (v. 8); a scroll in the hands of the one seated on the throne (5:1); seven seals on the scroll (v. 1); a slaughtered lamb (v. 6); harps and golden bowls of incense (v. 8); and thousands and thousands of

> The Revelation stories yet to be told all begin in the gathering of local congregations. The Revelation is meant first and foremost for them. It is for the gathered people of God, then and now.

angels (v. 11). We have entered a realm that we have never seen before. In other words, we become aware of two places at once—our earthly dwelling and the heavenly realm. Worlds collide in time on the Lord's Day. Now we know *when we are* and we know *where we are*.

Revelation 6

We are introduced to the four horsemen of the Apocalypse, who are summoned to ride across the earth: the white horse of conquest (v. 2), the red horse of slaughter (v. 4), the black horse of poverty and famine (vv. 5-6), and the pale green horse of death (v. 8). What happens at the throne begins to have an impact on the earth. We have seen these hoofprints in our towns.

As the Revelation unfolds, we are taken to multiple locations: altars shielding slaughtered souls, the earth reeling under the wrath of commands, the sealed tribes of Israel, angels with trumpets and little scrolls, a dragon chasing a pregnant woman, the sea of chaos birthing beasts, the reaping of a harvest on earth, a prostitute riding on the back of a beast, a grand city in ruins, a wedding supper, a battle to end all battles, and a new city. Oh, the places we'll go in the Revelation.

We have entered a world where we stand in our hometown church and see worlds we didn't even know existed. The location of the reader is in the local church, but the action occurs on a stage that intersects heaven and earth. Note the freedom of the Apocalypse to move between a throne in heaven and a black horse of famine affecting food prices. We're in a tornado with images, colors, numbers, and characters—all spinning before our eyes. Where are we? We are standing among the gathered people of God beholding a vision that blesses those who read and hear it. Now we have reached the most important location question. Who are we with? In whose presence are we experiencing this?

Entrance: The Accompanying Presence

A story places us in a certain time, at a certain place, with certain people. Very few stories survive with one lone character. Given that the Revelation is a journey for the people of God, it is important to know who we are traveling with. The plot of the Revelation is also the plot of a worship service. We begin our corporate worship by naming the God in whose presence we have gathered. We invoke, invite, and declare that God is among us. In this section, we will review the identity of the God who is present in the Revelation.

Revelation 1: The Exalted Christ

In the opening chapter, we need two program guides. One is the terminology for the Roman emperor. The same exalted language used for this human on the world's most powerful throne is used to speak of the Christ that we meet in the Patmos vision. Titles such as "him who is and who was and who is to come" (v. 4), "the seven spirits" (v. 4), and "the Alpha and the Omega" (v. 8) are veiled references to the emperor. References to heavenly bodies also correspond to the religion of the empire. The people of God sitting in their seven churches are smiling as they hear the subtle craft of titles and descriptions for their God in the opening verses. It's as if John is saying, "We know who really occupies the throne as ruler of the kings of the earth, wink-wink."

The other program guide needed is the Old Testament. The vision that John sees requires some grasp of Daniel 7. Two characters in this apocalyptic prophecy are combined into one. We see the Ancient of Days and the Son of Man in one vision. Before John ever sees the vision, he hears a voice telling him to write what he sees and send it to the seven churches. In other words, this amazing figure's first words are on behalf of the seven churches. John turns and beholds one who is hard to describe. He wants to tell us what he sees, but how can he describe the indescribable? It's like a poet or photographer looking at a sunset. A poet may write about the sunset, but words cannot paint the colors. And a photo cannot compare with actually seeing the sunset firsthand. All anyone can do is try his or her best. And this is what John did.

Trying to describe this vision of Jesus stretches John's imagination: a man with a "voice like a trumpet" (Rev. 1:10), hair "white like wool" (v. 14, NIV), eyes blazing like fire (v. 14), feet "like bronze" (v. 15, NIV), a voice "like the sound of rushing waters" (v. 15, NIV), and a face "like the sun" (v. 16). John exhausts his mental thesaurus to come up with descriptions that do justice to the vision. He reaches for the "-est" words—brightest, whitest, loudest, strongest. The Christ who appears to John supersedes all his categories. He cannot find words to tell us what he sees. He can only hint at what this Christ is like. God cannot be contained in words. Words fail. They limit and confine experience to marks on paper. God always bursts the boundaries of our descriptions.

John's response to Christ is telling. "When I saw him, I fell at his feet as though dead" (v. 17). John collapses before the unimaginable. His heart stops. His breath sticks halfway up his windpipe. His legs buckle underneath him. He falls on his face before the incomprehensible.

The body of our Lord Jesus Christ, once stripped naked on a public cross, now robed in splendor; once with hair matted by blood, now with hair white as wool; once with eyes wearied by Gethsemane's prayer, now with eyes of blazing fire; once with nail-pierced hands and feet, now with hands that hold stars and with feet that glow like bronze; once with a voice that could barely whisper "forgive them" and "I thirst," now with a voice like an unstoppable ocean coming ashore; once with a face darkened by death, now with a face that makes the sun look like a dim bulb.

Jesus extends his right hand of blessing to relieve the frightened prophet. "Do not be afraid; I am the first and the last, and the living one. I was dead, and see, I am alive forever and ever; and I have the keys of Death and of Hades. Now write what you have seen" (vv. 17-19).

We have entered the presence of one whose power supersedes all thrones, rulers, and emperors. The story called Revelation occurs in the presence of this God.

Revelation 4: The One Who Sits on the Throne

Following the letters to the churches, a door opens in heaven and the people are able to follow John's gaze into heaven, where they see a throne. Similar to the prophets of old, John has been granted access into the heavenly council chambers, where the salvation of the world is being plotted. Micah, Ezekiel, and Isaiah have all been here before. Like mice in a corner, they quietly observed what was grander and greater than they had comprehended. The throne of Revelation evokes several images:

- The theophany of God in the Old Testament—Mount Sinai with thunder, lightning, and shaking earth
- The ancient thrones of prophetic imagination, where heavenly council is in session (Isa. 40)
- The present throne of Rome's empire, where life and death is dealt on a daily basis

The one who sits on heaven's throne is not immediately named or described except for a likeness to jasper and carnelian. Because this throned being is nameless, the readers are able to fill in the titles based on their own history. While the world may conclude that this is Caesar, the people of God know better. What we see is vivid activity occurring around the throne. Two groups attend the one on the throne. Twenty-four elders represent the people of God. A multiple of twelve usually represents God's people—12 tribes; 12 apostles; 12,000 in each tribe; 144,000 people. Along with the twenty-four elders are four living creatures, reminiscent of the cherubim and seraphim in the holy of holies. The four creatures are a lion, an ox, a man, and an eagle. Creation and creatures are represented before the throne.

> On the throne, at the center of everything that exists, is God. God is the hub that secures the spokes. God is the one in whom all things hold together.

On the throne, at the center of everything that exists, is God. God is the hub that secures the spokes. God is the one in whom all things hold together. God is the center of the atom and the hub of the universe. Remove God from the center, and the world comes unglued.

No wonder when we bow before other thrones, our world falls apart! We are entering a story, a time, and a space where the central character reigns over everything.

And the immediate activity that we are caught up in is worship. Like a rock thrown in a pond, waves of worship emanate from the throne. In concentric circles we see the worship of the four creatures, then the twenty-four elders, then the innumerable attending angels, then every creature in heaven and on earth and under the earth. The worship does not end until it reaches every being in all creation. Life pulsates from the one who sits on the throne.

Eugene Peterson writes,

Worship is a meeting at the center so that our lives are centered in God and not lived eccentrically. We worship so that we live in response to and from this center, the living God. Failure to worship consigns us to a life of spasms and jerks, at the mercy of every advertisement, every seduction, every siren. Without worship we live manipulated and manipulating lives. We move in either frightened panic or deluded lethargy as we are, in turn, alarmed by specters and soothed by placebos. If there is no center, there is no circumference. People who do not worship are swept into a vast restlessness, epidemic in the world, with no steady direction and no sustaining purpose.[1]

At this throne, the people of God celebrate. As they worship, the one who sits on the throne is finally named: "Holy, holy, holy, the Lord God the Almighty, who was and is and is to come" (Rev. 4:8). "Holy" is the term that designates God as unique, other, in a class with nothing

---

1. Peterson, *Reversed Thunder*, 60.

else. The one who sits on this throne is not comparable to any other ruler who has occupied any other throne. The term "holy" eliminates all comparisons to existing realities. No one is like this one. For this reason, the most frequent word in our hymns is the word "holy."

Holy, holy, holy! Lord God Almighty!
    Early in the morning our song shall rise to Thee.
Holy, holy, holy! merciful and mighty!
    God in three Persons, blessed Trinity!

Holy, holy, holy! all the saints adore Thee,
    Casting down their golden crowns around the glassy sea;
Cherubim and seraphim falling down before Thee,
    Which wert, and art, and evermore shalt be.

Holy, holy, holy! tho' the darkness hide Thee,
    Tho' the eye of sinful man Thy glory may not see;
Only Thou art holy—there is none beside Thee,
    Perfect in pow'r, in love, in purity.

Holy, holy, holy! Lord God Almighty!
    All Thy works shall praise Thy name in earth, and sky, and sea.
Holy, holy, holy! merciful and mighty!
    God in three Persons, blessed Trinity![2]

---

2. Reginald Heber, "Holy, Holy, Holy! Lord God Almighty," in *Sing to the Lord* (Kansas City: Lillenas Publishing Company, 1993), no. 2.

This classic hymn is straight from the imagery of Revelation 4. Worship is the act of *Entrance* into holy presence. It is the announcement of who rules the world. Worship is a politically subversive act, a revolutionary declaration, and a pledge of loyalty that supersedes all others. Worship is the recognition that we are in the presence of awesome otherness. Worship is the heartbeat of the universe, the pulse of all creation. In this scene, the songs of saints bestow honor and glory and thanks. Crowns are laid at the feet of the one who sits on the throne. And the final words of the scene in chapter 4 declare that this one on this throne has "created all things, and by [his] will they existed" (v. 11).

The radical prophetic message of Revelation 4 is that human rulers, with their empires, thrones, and power, do not occupy the center of existence. We are invited to worship the God who sits at the center of existence. No one can usurp this throne.

Koester writes,

The heavenly throne is the vantage point from which John wants readers to look out upon the world of human affairs. Popular culture in the world of the seven churches gravitated toward human centers of power. Public appearances of the emperor often featured him sitting on a throne and accompanied by a crowd of friends, advisors, and attendants. When the emperor traveled, communities would send representatives, sometimes dressed in white, to greet him and present him with golden crowns to show their recognition of his sovereignty. Those who approached the throne would prostrate themselves, sometimes even bowing down before the throne when the emperor was absent. . . .

. . . Emperors preferred to cultivate the impression that people sang their praises because their virtues were universally recognized and made them worthy of such honors. A throne of admirers could keep up a thunder of applause day and night, referring to the emperor and even to lesser kings as "gods." . . . By giving readers a glimpse of God's heavenly court, John presses Christians in the seven churches to see such popular displays of power as garish imitations of the true sovereignty that belongs to the Creator, who alone is truly worthy of being called "Lord and God."[3]

The plot of the Revelation begins by locating us in three successive scenes: we are exiled in the presence of the risen Lord on the Sabbath, we are in the seven churches where the messengers of God have come bearing news, and we are before the throne of the one who created all things. We are meant to find our center here. While the dragons and beasts are coming, they do not control the narrative. They are ancillary to it. They will appear on stages that have already been graced by the worship of the one who sits on the throne.

Revelation 5: The Slaughtered Lamb

The sequence of Revelation 4 and 5 is the heart of the entire Apocalypse. While written as two visions, each falls into the other in a way that makes them one. The clue that the tornado is on the move is the oft-used apocalyptic phrase "after this I saw" or "then I looked." Two controlling images are being presented side by side—the holy one who

---

3. Craig R. Koester, *Revelation and the End of All Things* (Grand Rapids: Eerdmans, 2001), 75.

sits on the throne who is the Lord God the Almighty *and* the slaughtered Lamb.

The two images could not be more different: one acting, the other acted upon; one sitting in power, the other suffering in death; one sovereign, the other suffering; one alive as alive can be, the other dying as death can deal; one blessing, the other bleeding.

We are introduced to the character of the slaughtered Lamb by way of the scroll that is held in the right (sovereign) hand of the one who sits on the throne. It is imagined that this scroll is the Revelation, the Apocalypse to be uncovered, which will speak of the future of the churches. The scroll is sealed with seven seals. Ancient documents were rolled and secured by dripping wax along the seam of the scroll. The sender of the scroll authenticated the message by pressing a ring imprint into the soft wax. Only authorized persons could break the seal and open the scroll.

An angel inquires of the whole world, "Who is worthy to open the scroll and break its seals?" (5:2). A search is made in all of creation. No one is found. John, our Patmos writer, reenters the picture and weeps at the news that no one is found who is worthy to open the scroll (v. 4). This is a dead-end apocalypse if the revelatory scroll is unopenable and unreadable. Then one of the elders announces that there is one who is worthy.

The introduction of the worthy one is steeped in messianic expectation. The elder says, "Do not weep. See, the Lion of the tribe of Judah, the Root of David, has conquered, so that he can open the scroll and its seven seals" (v. 5). Judah is the tribe to which kings are born. As told in Genesis 49:9-10,

> Judah is a lion's whelp;
>> from the prey, my son, you have gone up.
>
> He crouches down, he stretches out like a lion,
>> like a lioness—who dares rouse him up?
>
> The scepter shall not depart from Judah,
>> nor the ruler's staff from between his feet,
>
> until tribute comes to him;
>> and the obedience of the peoples is his.

Exhibit A of the Judah kings is David, the model of messianic expectation. When the elder makes the announcement, our expectations are elevated by this résumé. It speaks of Jewish history, military strength, and global recognition.

What we see next is the essence of the paradox that is God. We hear one thing in the announcement of the elder and see quite another with our John-guided eyes. There, between the throne and the representatives of all creation, standing among the elders, we see a Lamb, appearing as if it had been slaughtered. Yet it has "seven horns [a symbol of total power] and seven eyes, which are the seven spirits of God sent out into all the earth" (Rev. 5:6).

The slaughtered Lamb is no stranger in our larger story. We remember the sacrificial lamb of Egypt's Passover. We remember Isaiah's Suffering Servant, who is led as a sheep to be slaughtered for our transgressions. We remember the Gospel of John's Lamb, who comes to take away the sin of the world. We have seen this Lamb many times in our story. Our problem is that we rush quickly to enthrone the slaughtered Lamb at the right hand of the Father so that we can get suffering in the rearview mirror. The Revelation offers us the Christ who cannot be separated from crucifixion. He stands among us as the slaughtered Lamb. This is not a past piece of his résumé; it is his ongoing identity.

The interplay of these two images is the tension that makes Revelation captivating. Lines are drawn between ruling and suffering, between reigning and dying, between empowerment and powerlessness. Which do we lay claim to? Both. In the nature and character of the God, who is revealed to us in Christ, we hold in tension things the world would never put together. At the throne of the Roman emperor, it is rule or be ruled, but not both. At the throne of God, it is both.

> **The God into whose presence we are ushered in the Revelation is both almighty God on the throne and the slaughtered Lamb.**

The God into whose presence we are ushered in the Revelation is both almighty God on the throne and the slaughtered Lamb. They are two, yet one; and the consistent mention of the seven spirits before the throne allows us to complete our Trinitarian understanding of the God. Lest we miss the "God-ness" of the Lamb, we immediately see the worship offered to the one on the throne in Revelation 4 repeated and offered to the Lamb in Revelation 5.

> When he had taken the scroll, the four living creatures and the twenty-four elders fell before the Lamb, each holding a harp and golden bowls full of incense, which are the prayers of the saints. They sing a new song:
>
> "You are worthy to take the scroll

>   and to open its seals,
> for you were slaughtered and by your blood you ransomed for God
>   saints from every tribe and language and people and nation;
>   you have made them to be a kingdom and priests serving our God,
>   and they will reign on earth."

Then I looked, and I heard the voice of many angels surrounding the throne and the living creatures and the elders; they numbered myriads of myriads and thousands of thousands, singing with full voice,

>   "Worthy is the Lamb that was slaughtered
>   to receive power and wealth and wisdom and might
>   and honor and glory and blessing!"

Then I heard every creature in heaven and on earth and under the earth and in the sea, and all that is in them, singing,

>   "To the one seated on the throne and to the Lamb
>   be blessing and honor and glory and might
>   forever and ever!"

And the four living creatures said, "Amen!" And the elders fell down and worshiped. (Vv. 8-14)

The pairing of these visions is necessary for a full understanding of the character of God. The divine holy one of the Revelation rules from a throne by suffering love, by sacrificial death, by painful participation in creation's chaos, by standing among the persecuted peoples, by going into the pits that humans die in. We are in the presence of one whose use of power is radically different from anything we have seen in the empire. We are in a narrative that sees the world through strange eyes and responds in strange ways. God rules through the slaughtered Lamb. And this will change the way we see the world.

Michael Gorman writes,

> Human beings, even apparently faithful Christians, too often want an almighty deity who will rule the universe with power, preferably on their terms, and with force when necessary. Such a concept of God and of sovereignty induces its adherents to side with this kind of God in the execution of (allegedly) divine might in the quest for (allegedly) divine justice. Understanding the reality of the Lamb as Lord—and thus of Lamb power—terminates, or should terminate, all such misperceptions of divine power and justice, and of their erroneous human corollaries.[4]

One of the reasons that the American church has failed to grasp the essence of the Revelation is that our national story is one of conquest. We have faced our enemies with equal or greater force and have conquered. Rarely have we needed to suffer. I say this of our dominant ruling class, not of the slaves and immigrants and poor who have suffered aplenty. The Revelation has been interpreted by those who hold power as a guidebook to winning. In the words of one preacher, "You better listen to the Lamb or you'll be gobbled up by the Lion." The thought is that the suffering of Jesus is finished and we are now in charge. Those who do not bend to our demands will face the judgment of a ferocious lion.

---

4. Michael J. Gorman, *Reading Revelation Responsibly: Uncivil Worship and Witness: Following the Lamb into the New Creation* (Eugene, OR: Cascade Books, 2011), 111.

Koester observes that the Romans expanded their empire by destructively conquering, enslaving, and thus excluding from citizenship and any sacred function "people of many tribes, languages, and nations." By contrast, "the Lamb conquers by faithfully enduring death" in order to bring "people of every tribe, language and nation" into "God's kingdom," where they can all serve as priests to God.[5]

I wonder if the poor have not been better recipients of the Revelation than the powerful. They understand life on the bottom of the power pile. They know what it is to be void of status and belonging. They have tasted their own frailty and weakness. From this social position, they can embrace the God who rules from a throne and yet participates in their suffering and gives them the dignity of belonging.

Other God-Lamb Sightings in the Revelation

We are not done with the God on the throne and the Lamb. They continue to make appearances as the tornado moves forward. We will revisit the throne scene, its worship, and its main characters several times (Rev. 7:9-14; 8:1-3; 11:15-19; 14:1-5; 15:2-8; 17:13-14; 19:1-10; 21:22–22:5). This enthroned Deity is the stabilizing reality of every challenge, every story, every twist and turn of Revelation's tornado.

Conclusion to the Entrance

So we enter our plotted story. We are aware of the time we have entered—exile from Rome. We know the place we live—our seven cities. We have entered the presence of a specific God who is known and understood through the image of a slaughtered Lamb. The

---

5. Koester, *Revelation and the End*, 79-80.

juxtaposition between our towns and heaven's throne gives us cause for a new imagination. As the seals of the scroll are opened, our story will unfold. The tornado is whirling around the center of everything and beginning to move forward. *Bad News* is on the horizon.

Prayer

Gracious God, we exist in time and space
because you have granted us life and breath.
You draw us together in worship that our lives may be centered on you.
Without a center, our life is fragmented.
We don't know who or whose we are.
We become slaves of technology who spend all our time at work.
We become slaves of pleasure who spend all our time at play.
We become slaves of boredom who spend all our time
with mind-numbing television and computer games.
Without you as our center,
we are scattered in every direction without meaning or identity.
We don't know where we are.
Morning fog becomes life fog.
We live in anxiety and fear.
Our life has no boundaries.
We chase advertisements, seductions, and pagan pied pipers.
We manipulate and are manipulated.
We stuff our souls with numbing placebos.
We are caught up in the latest diet fad, the newest car,
the fastest computer, the trendiest restaurant, the hottest movie.
Our life has no center. We are dislocated.

Call us to the center where you exist as holy, worthy, and loving.
And may we find our dignity as humans at the foot of your throne.
Thanks be to the one who sits on the throne
and the Lamb who has redeemed us.
Amen.

4

The Bad News and the Good News

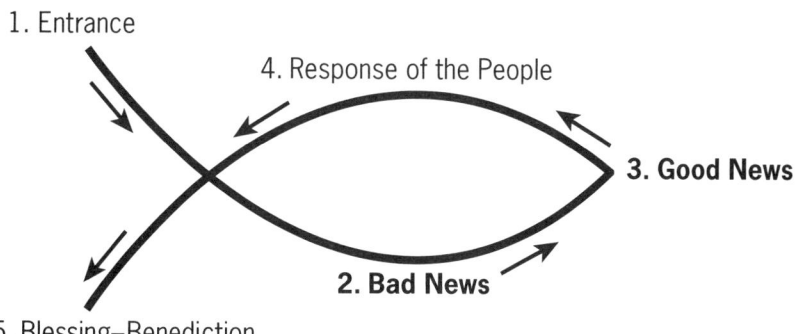

Isaiah found himself in a scene similar to the Revelation 4 throne room. He described it like this:

> I saw the Lord sitting on a throne, high and lofty; and the hem of his robe filled the temple. Seraphs were in attendance above him; each had six wings: with two they covered their faces, and with two they covered their feet, and with two they flew. And one called to another and said:
>
> "Holy, holy, holy is the LORD of hosts;
> the whole earth is full of his glory."

The pivots on the thresholds shook at the voices of those who called, and the house filled with smoke. And I said: "Woe is me! I am lost, for I am a man of unclean lips, and I live among a people of unclean lips; yet my eyes have seen the King, the LORD of hosts!" (Isa. 6:1-5)

This is the transition from *Entrance* to *Bad News*, from the presence of the holy God to the confession of uncleanness. What are people like us doing in the presence of a God like this? By what stretch of the imagination do we have the right to appear before this throne? Blazing holiness exposes everything that is not in keeping with the character of God. The purity of Trinitarian love uncovers every human motive and deed that is self-centered and self-serving. Sin is exposed. The empires of the world are critiqued. Emperors have no clothes to cover their lack of true sovereignty. Systems, powers, and ideologies are examined under the rubric of how humans are treated. And the only appropriate response is the confession of Isaiah: "Woe is me, and woe are the people I live among" (see v. 5).

> If our model is the holiness of God and likeness to the Lamb, then we are standing before a Grand Canyon gap between who we are and who God is.

The Revelation works the same way. The vision of God and the Lamb exposes the behavior of the people in the seven churches. It also stands in stark contrast to the ways of Rome's empire. If we measure ourselves only by the world that we live in, the Christian ethic is reduced to doing a little better, being a little kinder, and playing a little nicer than the big bad world out there. But if our model is the holiness of God and likeness to the Lamb, then we are standing before a Grand

Canyon gap between who we are and who God is.

When we gather for corporate worship, we invoke the presence of God and offer our worship in recognition of who God is. The very next thing we do is confess our sin, both personal and corporate. We recognize the distance between us and God. We admit that God's will is not being done on earth as it is in heaven. Between this holy God and people like us, there is a gap.

On our best Sundays, sin sits in the pews. Into the presence of this holy God, we bring our grasping anxieties, mouthy words about others, attitudes toward authority, marital frustrations and fissures, prejudices, tendency to nitpick people raw, festering wounds, misuse of power, bodily abuse, selfish posturing, lies of overestimation and flattery, secret dark places, preoccupation with image, and love of money. These things don't stick out in the world's shadowy lands, but put them under the blazing searchlight of the holiness of God, and they stick out like a Volkswagen on a Mercedes lot.

And if our *personal* hearts are clean and clear before God, then our *corporate* hearts still need to confess. None of us has graduated from praying the Lord's Prayer: "Forgive *us* [corporately and personally] *our* trespasses, as *we* forgive those who trespass against us."[1] In Isaiah's words, "I live *among a people* of unclean lips" (Isa. 6:5, emphasis added). We belong to and bolster systems that do great harm to others. Ours is a consumerist society with a demand for therapeutic cures to all that ails us. If we do not receive our fair share or our therapy, we sue. The litigious culture is so focused on individual rights that personal

---

[1]. "The Prayers," Daily Morning Prayer: Rite Two, in *The Book of Common Prayer* (New York: Seabury Press, 1979), 97 (emphasis added).

responsibility for others is left in the dust. In America, we sit as citizens of a land where babies are aborted, the gap between the haves and the have-nots is widening, the church is segregated, greed runs rampant, the environment is soiled, and entertainment is dehumanizing. I could go on. This is Bad News.

Stories require Bad News. You don't have a story until someone is in trouble. Nursery rhymes, novels, sitcoms, and the classics all feature someone in trouble. No sooner are we planted in "once upon a time" than we are introduced to characters who are in trouble: Goldilocks stumbling upon the home of the three bears, the creator of the Titanic declaring it unsinkable, the prodigal going forth with his fortune to assume control of his own life. We can see trouble coming early in the stories that capture our imagination.

This is true for all three literary genres that compose the Revelation. Apocalyptic is all about the dualism of good and evil, right and wrong, what God wills versus how the world is. Prophetic literature is occasioned by the actions of evil kings, greedy merchants, and enemy threat. Without human trouble, the prophets are silent. The New Testament Epistles are all written in response to community trouble—false teaching, immoral behavior, persecution, or compromise.

One of the primary connecting points between the biblical stories and the people in the pews is that in both places we find people in trouble. And when people are in trouble, they are interested in knowing how they might get out of trouble. Alternate ways of thinking and living are considered. People are willing to embrace new narratives, to live in other stories, as a means of escaping their current plot. Nothing opens us to change better than trouble.

Walter Brueggemann writes about our trouble in an article titled "Counterscript."[2] He makes the following points about our trouble and the hope offered in the gospel script:

1. Everybody has a script. . . .

2. We are scripted by a process of nurture, formation and socialization. . . .

3. The dominant script . . . is the script of therapeutic, technological, consumerist militarism. . . .

4. This script—enacted through advertising, propaganda and ideology, especially in . . . television—promises to make us safe and happy. . . .

5. That script has failed. . . .

6. Health depends . . . on disengaging from . . . the failed script. . . .

7. It is the task of the church . . . to detach us from that powerful script. . . .

8. The task of describing . . . is undertaken through the steady, patient, intentional articulation of an alternative script. . . .

9. The alternative script is rooted in the Bible and enacted through the tradition of the church. . . .

10. The defining factor of the alternative script is the God of the Bible, who, fleshed in Jesus, is . . . Lord and Savior of Israel and Creator of heaven and Earth. . . .

---

2. Walter Brueggemann, "Counterscript: Living with the Elusive God," *Christian Century*, November 29, 2005, 22-28.

11. ... We should not pretend that we have such an easy case to make in telling about this God. ...

12. The ragged, disjunctive quality of the counterscript to which we testify cannot be smoothed out. ...

13. ... The counterscript to which we testify is so disputed ... that its adherents are always tempted to quarrel among themselves. ...

14. The entry point into the counterscript is baptism. ...

15. The nurture . . . into the counterscript constitute[s] the work of ministry. ...

16. Ministry is conducted in the awareness that most of us are deeply ambivalent about the alternative script. ...

17. The good news is that our ambivalence . . . is precisely the primal venue for the work of God's Spirit.

The world forms our mental script. We live out a storied life. As Christians, we believe that there are only two stories in which we can live: the story of God resulting in life and the story without God resulting in death. And somewhere in our story, sin has made its mark. We have scripted patterns buried deep in our being. The formative culture that we grow up in provides us with scripts for each situation. These scripts are formed deep inside us as primal stories. We have scripts for fear, trust, low self-esteem, prejudice, greed, and safety. When we find ourselves in a given situation, we consult these scripts and enact the response called for by them. But these scripts originate from a world that is failed, broken, and death bound. There is no salvation in these scripts. Our imagination must be converted, reformed, and repatterned if we are to live out the script of the living God.

Revelation gives the people in the seven churches (and in our churches) new scripts, counterscripts, a new story, a God imagination, a Christian view of the world, a Lamb perspective. We cannot get to likeness to the Lamb unless we are willing to confront the Bad News of our situation. It is in knowing who God is that we come to understand how fallen we are. We begin in the presence of God, and then we move to uncover and confess sin as destructive of God's creatures and creation.

The moment we confess the Bad News, we are opened for the Good News. If you think about it, Bad News is required for Good News. The announcement that "the lost sheep is found" requires the precondition that the sheep is lost. The declaration that "Christ is risen" requires that Christ is dead and buried. The Good News that sin is now forgiven assumes that it wasn't before. Good News is the divine response to Bad News. Almost every story in Scripture finds someone in trouble. Noah is in the Bible because humans had filled the earth with violence. The father is depicted as waiting at the gate because the prodigal has gone off to squander his life. The letters of Paul are written because some troubling issue needs to be addressed in the church.

> Revelation gives the people in the seven churches (and in our churches) new scripts, counterscripts, a new story, a God imagination, a Christian view of the world, a Lamb perspective.

The Good News is gospel because it is the reaction of God to the destructive behavior of humans. And this divine reaction is the hook that we can hang our hopes on. It is the ground zero of our salvation. The distance between the Bad News and the Good News is where we find life.

We will turn now to explore the trouble of the Revelation. Sometimes it is rooted in the actions of the people in the seven churches. At other times it is the activity of a dragon or a beast. And sometimes the trouble is found in the judgment of God that moves arrogant people to repentance. With each appearance of Bad News, we are made ready to hear the Good News.

Revelation 1: Exile

It doesn't take long for us to recognize trouble on the horizon in the Revelation. No sooner does John complete his epistolary greeting than he shares his predicament. "I, John, your brother who share with you in Jesus the persecution and the kingdom and the patient endurance, was on the island called Patmos because of the word of God and the testimony of Jesus" (Rev. 1:9). Patmos is an island of exile where non-empire-approved persons are quarantined. It is an out-of-sight and out-of-mind place. Exile is the strategy of the empire against those whose voices make the citizens uncomfortable.

Usually in our story we encounter exile as a place we are sent: the children of Abraham down in Egypt, the conquered Israelites in Babylon, the church of Peter dispersed as a tiny minority among the pagans. Exile has often been home for the whole people of God. Here in the Revelation, John is the only character in exile. And he is there because the word of God and the testimony of Jesus do not have Rome's seal of approval. He was making people uncomfortable. Most likely he has been confronted in a local court, given the option to declare loyalty to Caesar, and ordered to disavow Christ. He has declined the offer.

We will see the recurrence of the phrase "faithful witness" throughout the Revelation. Jesus has already been introduced in 1:5 as "the faithful witness, the firstborn of the dead, and the ruler of the kings of the earth." In the letter to Pergamum, we meet the martyr Antipas, "my witness, my faithful one, who was killed among you, where Satan lives" (2:13). The saints around the throne are identified as faithful witnesses. In Revelation 11, we meet two witnesses who are attacked by "the beast that comes up from the bottomless pit" (v. 7). In Revelation 12:11, we hear the proclamation from heaven about those who have "conquered him by the blood of the Lamb and by the word of their testimony, for they did not cling to life even in the face of death."

It becomes clear to the Revelation reader that telling the story of God and the slaughtered Lamb is not welcomed. If we insist on doing this, we will be in trouble with the powers that allegedly rule the world. Exile is the consequence for John. There is a price to pay for swimming upstream against the empire. The Bad News is that the world does not welcome the only message that can save it.

Yet this Bad News is not the final word. In our story, Good News always follows Bad News. Our God responds to the work of evil. Our God shows up in exile. Our God never abandons the people who place their trust in the Lamb. The Good News here is that John, even though exiled on Patmos and hushed as a public witness to the Lamb, is not incommunicado. Jesus meets him there, and from Patmos comes this Revelation that is read in key cities along the Roman postal route, in local congregations where the people of God are gathered. Exile has never worked as a strategy for silencing the story of God. And it doesn't work here. God shows up in majestic glory in exile. Exile has not minimized the Lamb of God. It has not separated Jesus from his people. It has not ended the faithful witness. This is the gospel (Good News) of Revelation 1.

Revelation 2–3: The Situation of the Churches

Many have assumed that widespread persecution of Christians by the Roman Empire led to the composition of the Revelation. In truth, there was actually little public persecution of Christians by Rome on an empire-wide platform. The persecution was more local. In addition, the letters to the seven churches, while noting specific persecutions in Smyrna and Philadelphia, do not indicate persecution as the primary concern for the other five churches. In Ephesus, Pergamum, and Thyatira, the concern was the assimilation of the believers into the socioreligious cultural practices of the empire. In Sardis and Laodicea, the issue was complacency—the sloth that comes with wealth and position. Their trouble is as much internal as external.

N. T. Wright summarizes the letters to the churches in this way:
The seven letters . . . are sharp and pointed messages to the churches in question, and, through them, to the many other Christian groups already in the area—and to all others, then and now, who can listen in to what the risen Lord is saying. The letters all follow the same pattern. They begin with a reminder of some aspect of the description of Jesus in chapter 1. They continue by congratulating the church on what has been going well (only in Laodicea

is there nothing to praise), and then warning about what has been going badly (only in Smyrna and Philadelphia is there no fault to be found). The letters then end with a solemn warning and promise: the spirit is speaking to the churches, calling Christians to "conquer," and promising them some aspect of the glorious future which God has in store. . . . All the promises, and all the warnings, are for all the churches.[3]

Each letter is addressed to the angel (the defining spirit or ethos of the church) and begins with some characteristic of the exalted Son of Man before moving to the trouble in the church. We move from Entrance to Bad News with this shift from the Christ in whose presence we are gathered to the concern that God has for the church.

- To Ephesus, from "him who holds the seven stars in his right hand, who walks among the seven golden lampstands: . . . You have abandoned the love you had at first" (2:1, 4). Repent of your works (v. 5). The issue is assimilation into the culture, lacking a faithful witness.

- To Smyrna, from the one whose words are first and last, who was dead and has come to life: You are in poverty, you have been imprisoned, and you are being tested (vv. 8-10). The issue here is persecution, and the encouragement is to be faithful unto death.

- To Pergamum, from the one "who has the sharp two-edged sword": You are living in the shadow of Satan's throne, Antipas has been martyred, some are eating food sacrificed to idols and

---

3. N. T. Wright, *Revelation for Everyone* (Louisville, KY: Westminster John Knox Press, 2011), 11-12.

practicing fornication (pagan and empire temple practices), and you are holding to false teachings (vv. 12-15). The issue is clearly assimilation.

- To Thyatira, from "the Son of God, who has eyes like a flame of fire" and feet "like burnished bronze": You tolerate Jezebel, who beguiles you into fornication and eating meat sacrificed to idols (vv. 18-19). Again the issue is assimilation to and accommodation of the empire practices.
- To Sardis, from the one "who has the seven spirits of God and the seven stars": you are dead in your works; "wake up" (3:1-2). The issue is complacency. They bear no distinctive witness to Christ in their city.
- To Philadelphia, from "the holy one, the true one, who has the key of David" and opens where no one can shut and shuts where no one can open: You are being excluded and attacked by the synagogue of Satan, but I will open a door for you (vv. 7-9). The issue is persecution by local Jews who are taking offense at their refusal to participate in the socioreligious functions of the city.
- To Laodicea, from "the Amen, the faithful and true witness, the origin of God's creation": You believe you have everything you need and are rich and self-sufficient (vv. 14-17). The issue is complacency in their wealth and position.

Gorman, summing up the situation of the seven churches, observes that Christians in Asia Minor who associated in their daily lives with those "who did not share their conviction that 'Jesus is Lord'" had to decide whether they could be involved in pagan-related activities—such as attending athletic events, going to trade-guild meetings and parties, buying meat from pagan temples, and publicly recognizing the emperor's lordship and authority. Believers who chose not to participate were considered "by pagan nonbelievers . . . as unpatriotic and atheistic." Harassment, some informal and some formal, occurred in different localities, and this brought to mind "Nero's persecutions of the 60s" and "instilled fear in the Christian assemblies" that "led, in some assemblies, to increased accommodation."[4]

Let's drop in on a Christian family in Thyatira with an imaginary story of what the trouble in their world might have felt like.

Three Days in the Life of a Leatherworker: Revelation 2:18-29

Day One

It's Friday morning, the last day of the week in the Thyatiran business community. Stephen is up early, reading the Scriptures. Today he read the Shema, that great prayer of the Jews: "Hear, O Israel: The LORD is our God, the LORD alone. You shall love the LORD your God with all your heart, and with all your soul, and with all your might" (Deut. 6:4-5). The Jews at Thyatira First Church encouraged him to make that part of his worship. He has. Now the Shema is embedded in him: "The LORD is our God, the LORD alone." And so begins day one in the life of a Thyatiran leatherworker.

As the day dawns, he makes his way to his little shop. Stephen has been in business for two or three years. His specialty is horse reins. He has a friend named Bill who is a metalworker. Bill supplies the rings and the other metal parts that form the bridle and bit.

---

4. Gorman, *Reading Revelation Responsibly*, 31-32.

Stephen adds the leatherwork. He also makes sandals and belts, but horse reins are his strong suit. He has cornered the market.

The local leatherworkers' guild has been very good to Stephen. When he began business three years ago, they decided that none of them would compete with him and that they would refer all the horse reins to Stephen. They've kept their word, and his business has grown by leaps and bounds with the help of his brothers in the leatherworkers' guild. As a result, he is ascending to a new socioeconomic class. Although his own family was in the lower class, he is beginning to accumulate wealth that will take him places his father never dreamed of. Stephen and his wife, Mary, are beginning to enjoy the privileges of the upper middle class—and they like it. He has a pension plan, paid vacations, and a college savings account. His kids are going to attend TNU, Thyatira North Asian University.

Well, Friday's going well. It's a very busy day. Orders placed on Monday are ready by Friday. People come by the shop, pick up their orders, and pay. Everything is ready; he gives them what they ordered and collects.

Some of Stephen's friends from Thyatira First Church drop in to see how things are going. They comment on how well his business is going. "Yes, the Lord is blessing my business. See you Sunday."

Some of his friends from the leatherworkers' guild also drop by. "Are you going to make it to the big football game tonight?"

"Wouldn't miss it for anything!"

The Thyatiran Tigers are playing the Pergamum Panthers for the territory championship. And the leatherworkers' guild, of which Stephen is a member, is one of the key sponsors for the

Tigers. They bought a big block of tickets on the fifty-meter line. They sit as a group together and root the Tigers on to victory. The leatherworkers' guild provides the footballs for the games. It is part of their civic duty.

That evening Stephen and Mary go to the football game. Mary goes, but Stephen knows she doesn't like to. The football games are OK, but it's the fact that all those guild brothers sit together, drink too much beer, rabble-rouse, and launch some pretty foul language. Mary feels awkward sitting in the middle of it. Stephen would really rather not be there, but business is business. These are guild brothers, the guys who launched his business and send him referrals. If it weren't for these guild brothers, he probably wouldn't have made it as a leatherworker.

The game is exciting. The Thyatiran Tigers pull out a 20–16 win with a touchdown in the closing seconds of the game. Most of the guild heads to the bars, but Stephen and Mary make lame excuses about a long week and being tired, and they head home.

One of the guild brothers calls out, "See you tomorrow night at the weekly guild meeting."

Stephen responds, "I'll be there."

Day Two

Saturday is a laid-back day. Stephen sleeps in. When he gets up, he begins to work down through his honey-do list. It gets to midafternoon, and he thinks, *I want to get away for a little while. It's been a long week.* Stephen gets out his favorite camel and goes for a ride in the country with his son. They race and laugh and bond.

When he gets home, Mary says to him, "Stephen, Jezebel called while you were out and wants you to return her call."

Stephen replies, "Sure. Wonder what she needs?"

Jezebel is their Sunday school teacher, one of the finest Sunday school teachers they've ever had. She can draw things out of the text that no one else can see. She knows the deep secrets of God and has a charismatic personality. Under her leadership, the class is growing.

He calls. "Jez? Stephen here. Mary said you called while I was out camel riding. What can I do for you?"

"Well, Stephen, we're going to have four new couples in our Sunday school class tomorrow morning, and I thought it would be good for you to open the class and welcome these visitors. You're an up-and-coming businessman here in the community, and I'd like for these new couples, who happen to be part of my wool-workers' guild, to see a successful entrepreneur like you in front of the class."

Stephen agrees and consents to welcome the visitors. He hangs up and says, "Well, that's a first. No one has ever called on me to impress a visitor." Stephen smiles.

Mary asks, "Hey, what's the lesson about tomorrow?"

Stephen scratches his head for a moment and says, "It's something about our making a stance for Christ in the business community. Should be a good lesson."

"I wonder if an elephant will show up in the room again?"

"I don't know, Mary. Those ultraconservatives in the church who are bothered by guild membership just won't give it a rest. Lots of us belong to the guilds. Jezebel will probably address that. She can explain it in a way that doesn't bother people."

"We'll see," says Mary.

Saturday evening Stephen finishes supper and heads for the weekly meeting of the Thyatiran Leatherworkers' Guild. It is held at the Sardonian Temple every Saturday night. It is a mark of civic acceptance to be a card-carrying member of the Thyatiran Leatherworkers' Guild. He shows his membership card, goes to the closet where they store the sacred garb, takes his cloak, puts it on, and enters the big banquet hall. To one side is a huge slab of beef that has been barbecuing all day. The aroma fills the room. You can hear the laughter, revelry, and excitement of the gathering. They're talking about how business is going, about the quality of leather they're getting these days from Smyrna, and about the ball game last night. In a few minutes, the president of the guild bangs his gavel on the front table and says, "Come to order!" Everyone finds a seat. The president begins the ceremony by saying, "Let us honor the god Sardonus, who has prospered us in our business and given us health, wisdom, and success."

All the members stand, with hands placed on their hearts, and Brother Faustus comes up and says, "Bow for the prayer of invocation."

He begins to pray. "We praise you, O Sardonus, for your many kindnesses to us. We dedicate ourselves to your service to our dying day. Keep our brotherhood strong, our family ties healthy, and our guild united. Bless the cattle slaughter this year, and may the leather be top grade. We honor you, and we offer this side of beef as a sacrifice that would be pleasing to you. May you bestow your favor upon our sacrifice in the profit of our business. Bless our emperor, who establishes peace and rules over all in justice. We praise his lordship, the Caesar of the gods."

All the men resound, "Amen!"

The meal begins with the cutting and serving of the side of beef, and the aroma fills the room. About this time, they bring out the kegs of beer. Wine and beer begin to slosh throughout the hall. As these libations land in the stomachs, in the minds, and on the tongues of the men, the revelry and the party spirit increase accordingly. After a while, the meal is over. The men are pretty well sauced.

The president gets up again. "Fellows, the entertainment tonight is being provided by Murray's Leather Upholstery—and we all know when Murray has the program, it's gonna be good."

The lights dim, and two scantily clothed girls come out pushing a huge cake on rollers. And everyone knows who is in the cake and what she will do when she comes out.

Stephen thinks, *I've been looking for a good opening to slip out. This would probably be it, while the lights are dim.* And very quietly he slips out the side door, leaving his garb in the closet on the hook above his name. No one notices. As he moves down the road toward home, he hears in the background the revelry and the drunken roar. He knows they will be partying all night. Stephen gets home about midnight and quietly slips into bed beside Mary.

In her sweet, sleepy way she says, "Good guild meeting tonight?"

"It was OK," he responds evasively.

Day Three

Bright and early the next morning, the family is on their way to Sunday school. Stephen meets the new families and greets them. He asks how they happened to come, and they say, "Oh, Jezebel invited us. We're all in the same guild together, and she was telling us about the church and how it's growing. We wanted to check it out."

After Stephen has opened the class and greeted the guests, Jezebel says, "The lesson today is on standing for Christ in the midst of the business community." This should be interesting in light of the tension in the church about the guilds.

She begins by telling the class that there are three good reasons why it is permissible for Christians to belong to the guilds. "The first reason," she says, "is that these gods do not really exist anyway. We all know that they are fake. We know that there is no such thing as Sardonus. We are enlightened Christians, and we know that to pray a little prayer and offer a little sacrifice to a god that really doesn't exist doesn't do anyone any harm. And our enlightenment makes it OK for us to do this.

"Second, what better way to witness to the keeping power of the Holy Spirit in someone's life? For us to go to these guild meetings and be surrounded by sexual immorality and drunken revelry—for us to be there in the midst of all that and to keep ourselves pure is quite remarkable. And even if we do participate in the revelry, we know that it does not touch our minds or our spirits. We can compartmentalize our faith from our business necessities. We can keep our spirit pure and clean. What an awesome testimony to the keeping power of God!

"And third, if those ultraconservatives in the church are right and the devil is behind all this, we can be spies to infiltrate his ranks and learn the deep secrets of Satan. By knowing what the enemy knows, we will be able to defeat him."

Those are three good points. Stephen nudges Mary and whispers, "See, I told you it was OK. There isn't anything to it."

Jezebel adds one afterthought. "Besides," she says, "my husband is the treasurer of the church, and I happen to know that those of us who work in the guilds are the ones who keep the doors of the church open. We pay most of the bills. The other members work menial jobs for little pay. Our Sunday school class makes the most money. If it weren't for us, this church wouldn't survive."

And everyone says, "Amen." Class dismissed.

Stephen goes to Jezebel and says, "Jez, what a lesson! You can't believe how I needed to hear that this morning. You know, I've been struggling with this issue. To hear someone of your insight and capability teach in this way is a real help to me."

She replies, "Stephen, you are a rising star in this church!"

They move into the sanctuary for worship. The pastor begins the service with a serious tone. "Friends, I have a letter here from Brother John. You remember Brother John, who until two weeks ago was serving time on the island of Patmos. In his letter, Brother John tells me that he has seen the risen Lord. His description of our Lord is hard to imagine. As I read it, I was awestruck. And he says that the Lord gave him a letter for our church. I will read the letter this morning.

"You know there's been tension among us about guild membership. You know where I've stood on this. And what I read to you this morning doesn't come from me. John says it comes from Jesus, and I think we need to hear it. But I want to prepare you for what I'm about to read, because in this letter Jesus speaks very sternly to a teacher in our local church. And he says some things that, to be honest, are quite frightening. He is calling us to repentance, or else he will come and judge. I don't want to minimize the struggle that many of you are facing. I realize we are talking about your jobs, your businesses, and your careers. But I think it would be wise for us to hear what Jesus has to say."

Stephen tightens his grip on Mary's hand as they sit and listen. The pastor reads Jesus's letter from Brother John.

To the angel of the church in Thyatira write:

> These are the words of the Son of God, whose eyes are like blazing fire and whose feet are like burnished bronze. I know your deeds, your love and faith, your service and perseverance, and that you are now doing more than you did at first.
>
> Nevertheless, I have this against you: You tolerate that woman Jezebel, who calls herself a prophet. By her teaching she misleads my servants into sexual immorality and the eating of food sacrificed to idols. I have given her time to repent of her immorality, but she is unwilling. So I will cast her on a bed of suffering, and I will make those who commit adultery with her suffer intensely, unless they repent of her ways. I will strike her children [her followers] dead. Then all the churches will know that I am he who searches hearts and minds, and I will repay each of you according to your deeds.
>
> Now I say to the rest of you in Thyatira, to you who do not hold to her teaching and have not learned Satan's so-called deep secrets, "I will not impose any other burden on you, except to hold on to what you have until I come."
>
> To the one who is victorious and does my will to the end, I will give authority over the nations—that one "will rule them with an iron scepter and will dash them to pieces like

pottery"—just as I have received authority from my Father. I will also give that one the morning star. Whoever has ears, let them hear what the Spirit says to the churches. (Rev. 2:18-29, NIV)

You could hear a pin drop in the sanctuary. There are tears in Mary's eyes as she looks at Stephen. And Stephen sits there, looking ahead with a blank stare on his face. His mind is reeling as he thinks, *It's economic suicide. It would mean Chapter 13 for my business. It would mean social rejection in the business community. It would be a slap in the face to the guild brothers. It's a stupid business move.*

But he cannot escape the eyes of Jesus in the letter, the blazing eyes of fire that search the heart and the mind. He feels those eyes boring into his soul, and he realizes that he is naked and bare, defenseless with his reasoning in the presence of the risen Lord. And there is the direct reprimand, "Repent, or I will bring sickness and death as a judgment upon you." This isn't a suggesting Jesus who says, "Let's do lunch and talk about it." He's left no room for discussion. He says, "Repent now, or I will come in judgment."

Stephen ponders, *I do want to have a share in that great reign of Jesus when he comes—when his bronze feet crush the worship of Sardonus like fragile pottery. I don't want to be holding a guild cup. I want to share in that day of glory that comes as the bright and morning star. I want to be a part of his kingdom, but it's economic suicide.*

And they go home. Stephen plays with his lunch on the third day in the life of a Thyatiran leatherworker. He can't eat. That afternoon he says to Mary, "I think I'm going to take a long walk."

Stephen strolls the streets accompanied by his questions. *Does Christianity—and in particular does Jesus Christ—have the right to dictate my career? Are there some jobs that a Christian just can't do? Is my upper-middle-class goal appropriate to Christianity? Does it trump obedience to God?* Stephen feels the piercing eyes of Jesus boring into his soul. He asks himself, *Is my own enlightened liberalism nothing more than a proud sin in the eyes of Jesus Christ? Have I convinced myself of business practices that I know are wrong, all for the sake of making money and being accepted in the business community? Does Christianity conform to my job, or does my job conform to Christianity? Which shapes which? Am I the kind of Christian that a businessman ought to be? Or am I the kind of businessman who tries to be a little bit Christian? What is it in me that makes Jezebel sound so rational and so reasonable? Why do I want to agree with her? Why do I seek out teachers who say what I want to hear? And why is Jesus so stern about this? Why does he call for such costly obedience? He knows that if I do this, my business will suffer.*

Stephen sits with Mary late Sunday evening and says to her, "Honey, tomorrow morning I'm going to send a letter of resignation to the leatherworkers' guild. I can no longer compromise my loyalty to Jesus. I've not been clear about the issue until now. But honestly, as I view myself, I've obeyed the commands of Jesus that were convenient. I've obeyed the ones that didn't cost me anything. I've gotten fuzzy and apathetic in my witness, and I think I'm even a little proud of my enlightened position on what a Christian can do in the midst of the world.

"And, honey, do you know what brought me to this point? It's not your gentle nagging, even though you've been so kind to pray for me. It's not the conservatives down at the church. And it's not even the preacher's messages. It's those eyes of Jesus—those eyes that see through my rationale, through my enlightenment, through Jezebel's teaching, through my materialism, and through my motives. It's those eyes that see my heart. I can't escape them. And this afternoon when I was walking, not only did he see me, but I also saw him. And I looked into his eyes, and I saw there a divine mixture of disappointed love, righteous anger, and helping mercy. And I repented. It won't be easy—vacations, college, the middle class. I don't know. But my mind is made up."

And Mary says, "Stephen, you've got ears that hear what the Spirit said to the church this morning. Let me offer a prayer for us. Father, in this moment of quiet meditation, before a word that has shaken us, a word that shakes everything that is not rooted in you—before this kind of word, we pause. Even now, we find ourselves under the gaze of the eyes of Jesus—those eyes that see past everything, those eyes that bore deeply into our hearts, those eyes that see and know what we're willing to do to make a buck and why we're willing to do it, those eyes that see our desire to be esteemed and accepted by those whom we work with. You see us, Lord. Now grant us, we pray, enough courage to align our lives to your will and enough strength to bear faithful witness."

Gorman concludes about the seven churches that although Revelation is critiquing the empire's religion, injustice, and idolatry, it is not responding to an extensive persecution of Christians. It is best understood "as a response to 'ordinary empire,' to everyday evils, injustices, and misguided alliances that are daily with us."[5]

---

5. Ibid., 33.

For those of us who have taken an arm's-length approach to the Revelation, believing that we are dealing with a futuristic timetable and mysteries of antichrists, we must wake up. We have been located by the Spirit in this story. This Spirit still speaks through the Revelation to the church about our way in the world. The Bad News is that we are often accommodating of ways that do not bear witness to the Lamb. We are then assimilated into the worship of the gods of the empire. We next become complacent with their trinkets as we participate in the world's success rather than the Lamb's suffering. It is time for Christians to hear what the Spirit is saying to the church.

> **For those of us who have taken an arm's-length approach to the Revelation, believing that we are dealing with a futuristic timetable and mysteries of antichrists, we must wake up. We have been located by the Spirit in this story.**

The Good News of Revelation 2–3 is that God knows where we live and is aware of the empire that threatens us, seeks to assimilate us, and numbs us into disobedient complacency. This God offers three important things in the letters:

1. *Affirmation and Encouragement.* "I know your works, your toil and your patient endurance" (2:2). "I also know that you are enduring patiently and bearing up for the sake of my name" (v. 3). "I know your affliction and your poverty" (v. 9). "I know the slander [against you]" (v. 9). "You are holding fast to my name" (v. 13). "You did not deny your faith in me" (v. 13). "I know . . . your love, faith, [and] service" (v. 19). Again and again, God confirms the works and witness of his people. Sometimes, we

imagine God to be too much like Oscar the Grouch, only able to grumble about our shortcomings and failures. These seven letters have a heavy dose of affirmation and encouragement.

2. *Direct Command.* "Remember . . . from what you have fallen; repent" (2:5). "Do not fear what you are about to suffer" (v. 10). "Do not tolerate false teaching" (see vv. 20-22). "Hold fast to what you have" (v. 25). "Wake up, and strengthen what remains" (3:2). "Remember . . . what you received and heard; obey it" (v. 3). "Open the door, [and] I will come in to you and eat with you" (v. 20). God is not nebulous with us. If we are willing to hear what the Spirit says to the church, we will have all the instruction we need to move in the ways of God.

3. *Promise of Future Action.* "I will come to you and remove your lampstand from its place, unless you repent" (2:5). "I will give [you] permission to eat from the tree of life that is in the paradise of God" (v. 7). "Be faithful until death, and I will give you the crown of life" (v. 10). "I will give [you] some of the hidden manna, and I will give [you] a white stone, . . . [with] a new name [written on it]" (v. 17). "I will give [you] authority over the nations" (v. 26). "I will also give [you] the morning star" (v. 28). "You will be clothed . . . in white robes" (3:5). "I will confess your name before my Father and before his angels" (v. 5). "I will make you a pillar in the temple of my God" (v. 12). "I will write on you the name of my God" (v. 12). "I [will] spit you out of my mouth" (v. 16). "I reprove and discipline those whom I love" (v. 19). "I will give [you] a place with me on my

throne" (v. 21). God has not left us wondering about the future consequences of our present actions.

Revelation 6–7: The Seven Seals and the Horsemen of the Apocalypse

The coming vision is the first of five in the Revelation that are cohering narratives. They are each distinctive in offering a Bad News, Good News contrast. While there are connections between them, we get the sense that the tornado sets down, whirls in place for a time, and then lifts to move to the next vision. Debris (symbols and references) from one vision are often carried by the wind into the next story.

- Revelation 6–7: The Seven Seals and the Horsemen of the Apocalypse
- Revelation 8–11: Terrifying Salvation
- Revelation 12–15: The Evil Trinity: Dragon, Sea Beast, and Land Beast
- Revelation 15–19: The Prostitute, the Funeral of a City, and the Banquet
- Revelation 19–22: The Termination of Evil, Final Judgment, and the New Jerusalem

When you add the seven letters to the churches in chapters 2–3 and the vision of the throne of God in chapters 4–5, you have seven visions that compose the book, with an epistolary introduction and benediction in the first and last chapters respectively.

We ended chapter 5 with the global celebration of the Lamb, who is worthy to open the scroll. Our sense is that this is Good News and that with each successive seal, we will see the redeeming activity of God unfold. If heaven is rejoicing over the opening of the scroll, why should we not expect the victory of God and God's people? Right? Not exactly.

Each of the four living creatures before the throne summons a horseman. The first is the rider on the white horse, who represents the kings of the earth who go forth in military conquest. The second rider, on the red horse, removes peace from the earth and allows the enmity between humans to erupt into violence and slaughter. The third rider, on the black horse, represents economic depression, which impoverishes the poor while protecting the rich. Common food staples are exorbitantly inflated in price while the luxuries remain affordable. The poor cannot buy what they need for survival, and the rich are not inconvenienced in the purchase of their luxuries. The fourth horse is pale green, and its rider distributes death and the grave as the mop-up operation of the horses that have gone before—war, violence, and poverty.

This is not what we expected from the opening of the scroll. Destructive chaos is called forth by the living creatures and given permission to ride through the earth. Note that the power of the horsemen is passive. They *are given* authority; they do not possess this authority. We are looking at a mystery of the free God. Evil is given a leash to do its damage. Why? This is not the place for a full-blown theodicy that explains why evil exists in the presence of a holy God. But we would really like to know.

Resistance to the Lamb carries a heavy consequence. The world has established its own ways and they are deadly to the core. Gorman explains that judgment is the result of the world's unfaithfulness to God. It's "the inherent deadly" consequence of "deifying the non-divine," of rejecting "the divine gift of life."[6] Before God moves to judge this evil, God allows it to show its face. This is part of the judgment of evil by God. It is exposed for all humans to see, and we have the choice as free creatures to align ourselves with it or to oppose it.

N. T. Wright comments, "Unless the ills of the world are brought out, shown up in their true colours, put on display and allowed to do their worst, they cannot be overthrown. Unless the four horses ride out and do what they have to do, the scroll cannot be read. The victory of the lion-lamb will not be complete. . . . Things have to be exposed before they can be dealt with."[7]

This is a repeat of the cross of Jesus. In the cross, we see the dark actions of principalities and powers rise against the Lamb of God. Evil is fully exposed in the cross. We see its capacity to kill the innocent and to void the world of hope. It is only after evil has done its worst that God moves on the third day to judge evil and raise the dead body of Jesus.

The Revelation's horsemen are riding before the eyes of the seven churches. They know what the empire is doing in their cities. And many of them are suffering under this power. As the fifth seal is opened (6:9-11), we hear the saints, the martyrs who have made the ultimate sacrifice, as they cry out from beneath the altar that is before the throne. They are asking what suffering people have always asked. In the language of the lament psalms, their question is, "Sovereign Lord, holy and true, how long will it be before you judge and avenge our blood on the inhabitants of the earth?" (v. 10). They are given white robes

---

6. Ibid., 140.
7. Wright, *Revelation for Everyone*, 60-61.

and told to wait a little longer until the suffering of the people of God has come to completion. This is not the answer the seven churches would hope for, and yet it does assure them that those who have been martyred for their witness are neither forgotten nor unnoticed. They are under the altar, before the throne, in the presence of the God who promises a just judgment of the earth. The empire will not have the final word.

With the opening of the sixth seal (vv. 12-17), the judgment of God is unleashed in earth-shattering intervention. The sun blackens, the earth quakes, the full moon turns blood red, the stars of the sky fall to earth like ripe figs dropping from trees in a gale-force wind, the sky rolls up like a scroll, and mountains and islands are displaced. The judgment of God is more terrifying than the horsemen. "Then the kings of the earth and the magnates and the generals and the rich and the powerful, and everyone, slave and free, hid in the caves and among the rocks of the mountains, calling to the mountains and the rocks, 'Fall on us and hide us from the face of the one seated on the throne and from the wrath of the Lamb; for the great day of their wrath has come, and who is able to stand?'" (vv. 15-17).

This is terrifyingly good news. Evil will not go unjudged. The horses and their riders will not have the final word on humanity. God will respond in ways that shake the earth and cause all creatures to hide. No one can stand before the judgment of God.

Following the sixth seal there is an interlude (7:1-17) during which angels restrain the destruction of the earth while other angels mark the saints of God. They are sealed on their foreheads. In the same way that an author's signatory ring is pressed into soft wax assuring the ownership of the contents, the seal of God is placed on the people of God. The 144,000 symbolize all the people of God. Lest we are tempted to think of a narrow Jewish tribal nation or some limited denomination of the church, we are told that this is "a great multitude that no one could count, from every nation, from all tribes and peoples and languages" (v. 9).

As with other visions in the Revelation, when things get terrifying, we return to the hopeful throne scene of Revelation 4–5. The music from the throne flows again. "Salvation belongs to our God who is seated on the throne, and to the Lamb!" (7:10). John has remained at the throne and is asked by one of the elders if he knows who these 144,000 white-robed worshippers are. He is told that these are saints who have come through the great ordeal of the horsemen. They have washed their robes in the blood of the Lamb, and now they worship before the throne, sheltered from the empire by the one who sits on the throne.

> They will hunger no more, and thirst no more;
>> the sun will not strike them,
>> nor any scorching heat;
> for the Lamb at the center of the throne will be their shepherd,
>> and he will guide them to springs of the water of life,
>> and God will wipe away every tear from their eyes. (Vv. 16-17)

As the seventh seal is opened (8:1), there is silence in heaven for half an hour. The vision of Revelation 6–7 has come to an end. The tornado has touched down with apocalyptic horsemen, cries for justice, terrifying judgment, the sealing of the saints, and a return visit to the throne of God. Now that the whirling winds have moved on, we stand in awed silence at what we have just seen. The tornado lifts to move forward in its plotted path, but we are left to ponder what we have seen.

The Bad News and Good News play against one another. We live in a world where evil is given permission to do its work, and we are not immune to the wake of destruction. Some of us are martyred by it. All of us suffer. Evil cannot mask itself but is fully exposed for all to see. The creatures of God are given front-row seats to determine where their loyalties will be aimed. God has given us the freedom to side with the empire or with the Lamb. But the choice is clear. God marks those who belong to the Lamb. And they are assured that their life means something and that justice will be done. The view from the throne gives us courage to face the empire. It assures us of eventual justice and eternal joy. We are not abandoned in a world of wild horses. We are known, granted the freedom to choose, and marked as the children of God.

Revelation 8–11: Terrifying Salvation

We concluded the opening of the seven seals with a period of silence in heaven. The silence is short lived. Similar to the awe of a tornado that has finally moved off one spot and onto the next, we barely have time to consider the debris before the whirling wind drops down again, just down the road. Trumpets pierce the silence.

In the commencement exercise of Trevecca Nazarene University, where I serve as president, there is a tradition. The president marches through a bell tower, among the seated guests on the great lawn, down the aisle where the graduates will soon commence, and up to the podium. All of this is done in absolute silence. And then the silence is broken by the blaring of three trumpets. The transition from silence to blaring trumpets jolts the senses. It suggests that something impressive is about to occur.

In Revelation 8, we escalate from the terrifying horsemen to the trumpets of divine judgment. Similar to the way that God shook the empire of Egypt from sky to sea, God will shake the earth once again in judgment. As Peterson suggests, "The trumpet plagues reconstruct the Exodus plagues. The Exodus plagues were not punitive but purgative, sent not simply to make Pharaoh miserable, but to get him to change his mind, to repent."[8]

The judgments of God in the Revelation compose almost half of the book. We cannot rightly read the Revelation without coming to terms with the apparent dissonance. In Revelation 4–5, God sits on the throne, is celebrated as the creator who makes and sustains all things, and is worshipped by all creation. We see a God of order, life, and thriving. Yet we turn a few pages and we come face-to-face with the seven seals, the seven trumpets, and the seven bowls of wrath, each more destructive than the set of seven that preceded it. The tornado

---

8. Peterson, *Reversed Thunder*, 98.

of destruction is picking up speed and leaving the earth in shambles. While the point can be made that a rejection of God invites chaos to reign, the Revelation leaves no doubt that God is the instigator and power behind this destruction.

Many misreadings of the Revelation find in this scenario ample justification for a futuristic theology that destroys the earth. And in the section we are about to study, they also find assurance to the faithful that they will be protected from this cataclysmic destruction of the earth. Putting these two together, they draw the opinion that the judgment of God will destroy the earth but that believers will be raptured before this occurs. The earth becomes the final hell as it is dismantled by the one who created it, and those who have rejected the Lamb are destroyed right alongside.

This could not be further from the truth. When you hear popular millennial theories suggesting that God is going to abandon creation and leave evil to rule over it, be highly suspicious! Does a man restore a 1967 Mustang and loan it out to a demolition derby driver for the weekend? Does a woman carry a child in her womb for nine months and then ask a gorilla to watch it while she goes to the store? Does God sit in the center of the universe, holding it together, and ask evil to take the reins? I don't think so. Let me explain.

The Scriptures consistently depict God as saying, "The earth is mine." We find no references to a God who is willing to concede creation to evil. In Romans 8 we read,

> I consider that the sufferings of this present time are not worth comparing with the glory about to be revealed to us. For the creation waits with eager longing for the revealing of the children of

God; for the creation was subjected to futility, not of its own will but by the will of the one who subjected it, in hope that the creation itself will be set free from its bondage to decay and will obtain the freedom of the glory of the children of God. We know that the whole creation has been groaning in labor pains until now; and not only the creation, but we ourselves, who have the first fruits of the Spirit, groan inwardly while we wait for adoption, the redemption of our bodies. For in hope we were saved. Now hope that is seen is not hope. For who hopes for what is seen? But if we hope for what we do not see, we wait for it with patience. (Vv. 18-25)

All of creation groans for the redemption and restoration of the earth, even as our dead bodies long for resurrection. The Revelation itself rejects the total destruction of the earth. In chapter 21, the new Jerusalem comes down to earth and initiates the new heaven and earth. The temple of Revelation 22 is on the earth. The victorious Lamb stands on the earth as heaven declares that "the kingdom of the world has become the kingdom of our Lord and of his Messiah" (11:15).

The stories of judgment do not make up a time line of the sequential destruction of the earth. For instance, during the sixth seal, the heavenly bodies all disappear, but by the third and fourth trumpets, they are back again. The grass is completely burned up in one judgment, but a few trumpets later, this same grass is protected from the devouring locusts. The series of judgments are not sequential and permanent. They are images of judgment that depict the activity of God to bring an idolatrous creation to its knees in repentance.

In addition, while the interludes between the sixth and seventh seals and the sixth and seventh trumpets depict protection, divine care, and an escape from the terrifying judgment, in no way do they suggest that believers will not suffer as the earth is judged. The faithful martyrs are under the altar before the throne of God asking for justice in Revelation 6. The two witnesses are martyred in Revelation 11. In both interludes of reprieve for the people of God, suffering is present. To concoct from these texts a rapture from judgment is to ignore the primary biblical understanding of God's relation to the earth. It nullifies the way of the slaughtered Lamb, who redeems the world by participating in its suffering.

The judgment narratives are about our salvation, which makes them Bad News that has Good News embedded in the same events. I have not always liked the word "judgment." It was too harsh, too condemning. But I am learning better. The judgment of God is our salvation. The word does not mean simply damnation, nor is it a synonym for "condemnation." God's judgment is a righteous verdict, a divine evaluation, and a heavenly decree. It is God's order to bring things that are wrong to an abrupt halt and to let our lives be exposed to the eyes of the one who sits on the throne. Only such exposure to God's understanding of worship can save us.

> **The judgment narratives are about our salvation, which makes them Bad News that has Good News embedded in the same events.**

The best parable of salvation by way of judgment that I have seen comes from a story told by Barbara Brown Taylor. During her stay on an island Barbara observed one evening a turtle laying her eggs on the beach. She left the turtle alone and returned the following day. The turtle was gone, leaving its tracks in the sand. Unfortunately, the turtle was headed away from the sea and toward the sand dunes "already hot as asphalt in the morning sun."

Barbara followed the tracks and found the turtle, worn and overheated. She then located a park ranger, who brought his jeep. The ranger flipped the turtle on her back, secured her front legs with chains, and hitched the chains to the jeep. He then "took off, yanking her body forward so fast that her open mouth filled with sand and then disappeared underneath her as her neck bent so far" that it looked as if "it would break." After dragging the turtle behind the jeep to the beach, the ranger removed the chains. The turtle lay still in the water until several waves washed over her and revived her. Reflecting on the turtle's rescue by way of a "nightmare ride through the dunes," Barbara observed "that it is sometimes hard to tell whether you are being killed or saved by the hands that turn your life upside down."[9]

In summary, the visions of judgment in the Revelation are not out of character with the one who sits on the throne. They are, instead, an expression of God's intent to save all creation. The scenes of destruction are not to be taken literally. They are symbols of a God who shakes an idolatrous world into humble recognition of its waywardness. Judgment is not God's last act but rather God's early move to redeem us.

What conclusions might the seven listening churches come to? They are not to have loyalty to an empire that is coming apart at the seams. They are not to worship rulers that are powerless to stand before the God who shakes the earth. They are not to worship powers that are

---

9. Barbara Brown Taylor, "Preaching the Terrors," *Leadership Journal* (Spring 1992): 45.

doomed. They are not to compromise with cults of idolatry. They are to have only full and total allegiance to the Lamb.

Let's walk through Revelation 8–11. Trumpets are given to seven angels. Another angel casts fire from the altar onto the earth. The earth is startled to alertness by the impact of the shaking—thunder, lightning, and earthquake. If this has not alerted everyone that something is about to occur, the first trumpet shatters the short-lived silence of heaven as hail and fire burn up a third of the earth, a third of the trees, and all of the green grass. Interestingly, in most depictions of divine judgment, only fractions are used. The destruction is neither final nor total, but fractional. The second trumpet results in a burning mountain being thrown into the sea causing a third of the sea to become blood, a third of the sea creatures to die, and a third of the ships to be destroyed. Fractions are used again. With the third trumpet a star named Wormwood (bitter taste) falls from heaven and lands in the rivers and springs, making them bitter enough to kill. Following the fourth trumpet, a third of the sun and moon and stars are struck, causing darkness during a third of the day.

Similar to the seven seals in Revelation, these first four trumpets are grouped in the same way as the four horsemen. We get a break as an eagle warns us, "Woe, woe, woe to the inhabitants of the earth, at the blasts of the other trumpets that the three angels are about to blow!" (8:13). The last three trumpets are grouped as three woes that are yet to come. There is no letup of judgment in sight.

The fifth and sixth trumpets are miniscenes in themselves. The fifth trumpet introduces a star that falls to the earth and opens a shaft to the bottomless pit. From this shaft comes thick smoke that darkens the sun and makes the air unbreathable. Out of the smoke come hordes of locusts that charge like horses, have faces like the faces of humans, teeth like the teeth of lions, hair like the hair of women, scales like iron breastplates, and tails with stingers like the tails of scorpions. And the sound of the locusts is like that of chariots rushing into battle. Their commander is Abaddon (or Apollyon), "the angel of the bottomless pit" (9:11). They are given authority to torture all "who do not have the seal of God on their foreheads" (v. 4). Their bite will not bring death but will cause the bitten to wish they were dead.

It would be interesting to try to draw this creature that emerges from the smoke of the bottomless pit. It is a conglomeration of symbols that strike fear into the human heart—darkness, scorpion stings, lions' teeth, and intense pain.

The sixth trumpet is no relief. The angels who had been restraining the winds of destruction are released. A two-hundred-million-horse cavalry is unleashed to kill a third of humankind. The horses have lions' heads, and they breathe out fire, smoke, and sulfur. Their tails are like snakes. From head to tail this cavalry of two hundred million kills with fire from their mouths and serpent bites from their tails. One third of humans die. Fractional destruction shows up again. This is terrifying.

With these six trumpets, people have been shaken to the core, burned, darkened, tortured, and killed. Certainly the judgment of God has moved humankind to turn from the idols, empires, and beasts of evil. Certainly repentance is on the horizon. Not so. "The rest of humankind, who were not killed by these plagues, did not repent of the works of their hands or give up worshiping demons and idols of gold and silver and bronze and stone and wood, which cannot see or hear or walk. And they did not repent of their murders or their sorceries or their fornication or their thefts" (vv. 20-21).

Following the sixth seal and the sixth trumpet, when it seems that the earth can take no more, there is a reprieve, an intermission of sorts. After the sixth seal, the people of God are marked with the seal of the Lamb and gathered at the throne in worship. Following the sixth trumpet, we meet a mighty angel from heaven, "wrapped in a cloud," hooded by a rainbow (10:1). We cannot help but think of the story of Noah when God came to the brink of destroying every living thing. The flood was God's eraser, God's delete button. And God was down to one floating zoo from being done with his creatures who had filled the earth with violence. But God remembered Noah, and the waters began to recede. The story concludes with God placing a rainbow in the sky as a reminder, not to humans, but to God, that never again would he destroy the earth by flood. The angel of Revelation 10 is covered by the rainbow of this divine promise.

An angel reminds us in Revelation 10:6 that the God of judgment is still the God of creation, "who created heaven and what is in it, the earth and what is in it, and the sea and what is in it." This angel oath contains a promise of finality: "There will be no more delay, but in the days when the seventh angel is to blow his trumpet, the mystery of God will be fulfilled, as he announced to his servants the prophets" (vv. 6-7).

At this point, John of Patmos is reintroduced into the narrative. We tend to forget that he is always there as our guide and narrator but rarely spoken to or included in the action. John is told to take and eat the scroll that the angel is holding. We imagine this to be the scroll once held by the one who sits on the throne, now opened by the Lamb. Similar to the experience of the scroll-eating prophet Ezekiel, the scroll is sweet in his mouth but bitter in his stomach. Then he is told to measure the temple of God.

Measuring the temple suggests that God intends to preserve and protect the temple. Many have conjectured whether this signals a future rebuilding of the Jerusalem temple. It is more likely that this is a symbol of the people of God, the church, the community of the Lamb. God intends to preserve the function of his people in the world. We are reminded of the promise made to the overcomers of Philadelphia in Revelation 3:12: "I will make you a pillar in the temple of my God." In the new Jerusalem of Revelation 21, there is no temple. The dwelling of God is not in buildings made by hands, but among his people: "See, the home of God is among mortals. He will dwell with them as their God; they will be his peoples, and God himself will be with them" (v. 3). The New Testament texts regarding the temple do not suggest a rebuilding of an earthly structure. Rather, God dwells among us, and we are being built into a holy temple. We recall the words of Ephesians 2:19-22:

> So then you are no longer strangers and aliens, but you are citizens with the saints and also members of the household of God, built upon the foundation of the apostles and prophets, with Christ

Jesus himself as the cornerstone. In him the whole structure is joined together and grows into a holy temple in the Lord; in whom you also are built together spiritually into a dwelling place for God.

At this point in the interlude, we meet two witnesses who are given authority to prophesy. They wear sackcloth as a symbol of the repentance they preach. Similar to Moses and Elijah, they have the power to stop rain, turn water to blood, and strike the earth with plagues. Divine protection surrounds them during their 1,260 days of prophesying (42 months, or 3½ years, symbolic for a time of testing). At the completion of their mission, when their testimony is finished, the beast rises from the bottomless pit and kills them. Their bodies are dishonorably dumped in the street of the great city, called Sodom and Egypt. For three and a half days, the people gaze on their slaughtered bodies and refuse to allow burial. The inhabitants of the earth gloat over them in celebration. The repentance preachers are dead.

What are we hearing? The two witnesses are symbols of the faithful people of God bearing witness while they can. They are operating in the great city, which is the headquarters of the empire. We will hear more about the great city when the tornado drops us down in Revelation 17–18. This city is Sodom and Egypt and Babylon and Rome—all the places where the people of the Lamb have suffered and had their lives extinguished. The public humiliation of their displayed bodies is akin to the death of Jesus on the cross. The gloating of the inhabitants of the earth is akin to the soldiers and mockers before the cross of Christ. To the naked eye, it appears that the beastly empire has won.

The voices of the faithful witnesses of God have been stilled. The bodies of the two witnesses are abandoned to buzzards.

The remarkable shift from Bad News to Good News in the next verse reminds us of another gospel prelude to hope—"and on the third day" (Luke 18:33):

> But after the three and a half days, the breath of life from God entered them, and they stood on their feet, and those who saw them were terrified. Then they heard a loud voice from heaven saying to them, "Come up here!" And they went up to heaven in a cloud while their enemies watched them. At that moment there was a great earthquake, and a tenth of the city fell; seven thousand people were killed in the earthquake, and the rest were terrified and gave glory to the God of heaven.
>
> The second woe has passed. The third woe is coming very soon. (Rev. 11:11-14)

Here is something we have not seen. Apparently, the resurrection of the faithful witnesses does what the plagues of judgment did not do. At the end of the six trumpets, the people did not repent but continued to worship demons and idols. At the resurrection of the two witnesses, only seven thousand are killed and only a tenth (smallest fraction yet) of the city fell. *All the rest* gave glory to the God of heaven. We see a turning of people toward the creator Lamb. We are reminded of Elijah, who complained of only seven thousand who refused to worship idols. In the Revelation, all *but* seven thousand have repented and turned toward the living God.

We are now ready for the seventh trumpet, which is also the third woe. We have been promised in Revelation 10:7 that the mystery of

God will be fulfilled with the blowing of this trumpet. Will there be more silence in heaven as with the seals? Let's see.

> Then the seventh angel blew his trumpet, and there were loud voices in heaven, saying,
>> "The kingdom of the world has become the kingdom of our Lord
>>> and of his Messiah,
>> and he will reign forever and ever."
>
> Then the twenty-four elders who sit on their thrones before God fell on their faces and worshiped God, singing,
>> "We give you thanks, Lord God Almighty,
>>> who are and who were,
>> for you have taken your great power
>>> and begun to reign.
>> The nations raged,
>>> but your wrath has come,
>>> and the time for judging the dead,
>> for rewarding your servants, the prophets
>>> and saints and all who fear your name,
>>> both small and great,
>> and for destroying those who destroy the earth."
>
> Then God's temple in heaven was opened, and the ark of his covenant was seen within his temple; and there were flashes of lightning, rumblings, peals of thunder, an earthquake, and heavy hail. (11:15-19)

The judgment of God is bringing salvation to the earth. People turn to the Lamb, the faithful witness, the suffering Jesus, the crucified, the one risen from the dead. Ownership of the kingdoms of the world is now recognized as his, and he will reign forever and ever. Can you hear the "Hallelujah Chorus"? We are back in the throne room again, with the twenty-four elders singing praises. We find ourselves in the holy of holies, where the ark of the covenant resides. God's thick presence is with us in the struggle where we live. This is a quasi ending for the Revelation, a celebratory stop.

> The judgment of God is bringing salvation to the earth. People turn to the Lamb, the faithful witness, the suffering Jesus, the crucified, the one risen from the dead.

As the tornado lifts from this scene, we try to catch our breath and weigh what we have just seen. But John has gone on to the next vision of the whirling tornado.

Revelation 12–15: The Evil Trinity: Dragon, Sea Beast, and Land Beast

Revelation has two trinities. The Holy Trinity consists of the one who sits on the throne (God the Father), the slaughtered Lamb (God the Son), and the seven spirits before the throne of God (God the Spirit). The evil trinity is made up of the dragon (Satan), the beast of chaos out of the sea (rulers aligned with Satan), and the land beast-false prophet (the cultic priests that serve the interests of Satan). In Revelation 12–20, we will meet in succession the dragon (Satan), the sea beast, the land beast-false prophet, and the prostitute. In reverse order, we will see their defeat: first, the prostitute is defeated by the Lamb and consumed by the sea beast; then the false prophet is defeated, followed by the sea beast; and finally Satan is bound and cast into the lake of fire and is no more. They appear and then leave in reverse order.

The earlier visions have focused on earthly judgment. The coming visions focus on the destruction of those who destroy the earth (11:18). We are about to confront the powers behind the compromise and idolatry that the inhabitants of the earth have embraced. The evil empire has exercised power in many ways: the manipulation of force, called militarism; the manipulation of words, called spin or propaganda; the manipulation of money, called taxation; the manipulation of access to the marketplace, called guild membership; and the manipulation of pleasure, called hedonism. Our worldly assumption is that if the kingdom of God is going to defeat these principalities and powers, it must flex its muscles to exercise greater force.

Make no mistake, God's kingdom is about power, but not the kind of power that Rome exerts. Too often the church has fled to one of two strategies: either amass more power than Rome through the ballot box, political clout, wealth, or stardom or give up and settle for a safe little haven of fellowship, where believers can duck suffering and try to save a few souls while waiting for the rapture. Neither option works in the Revelation. God goes into the teeth of evil by enduring death as a slaughtered Lamb. Suffering is the path to victory and power. God's victory is won by the life, death, and resurrection of the Lamb. And God does not allow the church to shrink into an escapist theology but rather calls her to bear faithful witness in the streets of the great city, even to the point of martyrdom.

In our next vision, we see two openings into heaven (Rev. 12). Two figures appear, one in each opening. First, we see a woman whose clothes are woven of sunbeams. She stands on the moon and wears a crown of twelve stars. She is pregnant. We hear hints of Eve, Israel, and the church in this character. In short, she symbolizes the people of God. Next we see a great red dragon. He is as ugly as the woman is beautiful. His color denotes bloody slaughter. He has seven heads and ten horns, symbols of total power.

The woman is in labor with a child. This child will rule all the nations with a rod of iron. This is a messianic reference from Psalm 2. The child is Jesus, born out of Israel in fulfillment of the promise that the seed of Eve will bruise the serpent's head. The dragon licks his chops as he crouches, awaiting the birth of the child. He lunges and misses as the child is snatched away to the throne of God. The entire story of the birth, life, teaching, miracles, death, and resurrection of Jesus are telescoped into this one ascending move that takes the child to the throne of God. The woman escapes to the wilderness, where she is nourished by God for 1,260 days (42 months [or 3½ years]—a limited time of persecution).

We are hearing several story references all at once: the Hebrew children snatched out of Egypt and nourished by God in the wilderness, the ancient Roman story of the gods who birth an emperor who kills a dragon to establish a reign of peace, and possibly even the story of Herod seeking to kill the Bethlehem baby. Catch the geography. The woman is now fleeing from the dragon on earth. The child is ascended to the throne. The dragon is still in heaven accusing the saints before the throne of God.

War breaks out in heaven. Michael, the archangel of God, fights the dragon. In Revelation 12:9, the résumé of the dragon expands: This is "that ancient serpent, who is called the Devil and Satan, the deceiver of the whole world." The battle ensues, and the dragon is defeated, expelled from heaven, and cast down to the earth along with all his angels. The victory announcement is made:

Then I heard a loud voice in heaven, proclaiming,
> "Now have come the salvation and the power
>> and the kingdom of our God
>> and the authority of his Messiah,
> for the accuser of our comrades has been thrown down,
>> who accuses them day and night before our God.
> But they have conquered him by the blood of the Lamb
>> and by the word of their testimony,
>> for they did not cling to life even in the face of death.
> Rejoice then, you heavens
>> and those who dwell in them!
> But woe to the earth and the sea,
>> for the devil has come down to you
> with great wrath,
>> because he knows that his time is short!" (Vv. 10-12)

This heavenly victory is significant on several counts. The saints have participated in this cosmic victory by the "blood of the Lamb and by the word of their testimony" (v. 11). They have joined the Lamb in exercising power that defeats evil. Let all the churches along the Roman postal route hear this clearly. Victory is won by suffering love. Evil is defeated by the laying down of life. The dragon no longer has access to heaven, where he and his angels have contested God's rule and accused God's saints. Not only is the child Messiah enthroned, but also the chief nemesis is expelled. Satan is cast down to earth and limited like a caged animal. His defeat, his limitations, and his short leash of time make him even more ferocious.

As soon as the dragon-Satan hits the earth, he immediately pursues the woman who gave birth. But she is borne up on the wings of an eagle and escapes into the wilderness, where she is nourished for "a time, and times, and half a time" (v. 14)—again, 3½ years or 42 months or 1,260 days—a limited time of trial. The dragon spews a flood from its mouth to drown her (the Red Sea threat of Exodus), but the earth swallows the flood. Then the dragon stalks off to make war on the children of the woman—the church.

He marshals reinforcements that fill out the evil trinity. From the sea rises a beast with ten horns, seven heads, and ten crowns. The beast is quite odd, with the body of a leopard, the feet of a bear, and the mouth of a lion. The sea beast is given the authority and throne of the dragon for forty-two months (limited time). Similar to the slaughtered appearance of the Lamb, the sea beast has a head wound suggesting that it might have been killed. The beast blasphemes God, makes war on the saints, and conquers people. The saints are called to endurance in the face of this temporary onslaught. The whole earth follows the beast and declares that no one is like the beast and that no one can fight against it. We know better because we have just seen dragon power defeated by Michael and the saints. The world might be enamored with the power of this beast, but we who had a ringside seat in heaven know of a greater power.

In Revelation 13:11-15, we meet the third person of the evil trinity, the land beast:

> Then I saw another beast that rose out of the earth; it had two horns like a lamb and it spoke like a dragon. It exercises all the authority of the first beast on its behalf, and it makes the earth and its inhabitants worship the first beast, whose mortal wound had been healed. It performs great signs, even making fire come down from heaven to earth in the sight of all; and by the signs that it is allowed to perform on behalf of the beast, it deceives the inhabitants of earth, telling them to make an image for the beast that had been wounded by the sword and yet lived; and it was allowed to give breath to the image of the beast so that the image of the beast could even speak and cause those who would not worship the image of the beast to be killed.

This land beast is called a false prophet. Like a religious charlatan with tricks of power and deceptive signs, the false prophet seeks to deceive people. Many believe this false prophet refers to the priests and leaders of local cults where emperor worship and idolatry were practiced. They are the local presence of the empire, in the same way that the third member of the Holy Trinity, the sevenfold Spirit of God, is the immediate presence of God in the world. Just as the Spirit speaks to the gathered church, the false prophet speaks to the people who gather in guilds, cultic worship, and the temples of deities.

It is possible that John is using the humor of Isaiah here to poke fun at the thought that a carved image of deity could actually breathe and talk. Listen to the humor of the ancient prophet:

All who make idols are nothing, and the things they delight in do not profit; their witnesses neither see nor know. And so they will be put to shame. Who would fashion a god or cast an image that can do no good? Look, all its devotees shall be put to shame; the artisans too are merely human. Let them all assemble, let them stand up; they shall be terrified, they shall all be put to shame.

The ironsmith fashions it and works it over the coals, shaping it with hammers, and forging it with his strong arm; he becomes hungry and his strength fails, he drinks no water and is faint. The carpenter stretches a line, marks it out with a stylus, fashions it with planes, and marks it with a compass; he makes it in human form, with human beauty, to be set up in a shrine. He cuts down cedars or chooses a holm tree or an oak and lets it grow strong among the trees of the forest. He plants a cedar and the rain nourishes it. Then it can be used as fuel. Part of it he takes and warms himself; he kindles a fire and bakes bread. Then he makes a god and worships it, makes it a carved image and bows down before it. Half of it he burns in the fire; over this half he roasts meat, eats it and is satisfied. He also warms himself and says, "Ah, I am warm, I can feel the fire!" The rest of it he makes into a god, his idol, bows down to it and worships it; he prays to it and says, "Save me, for you are my god!" (Isa. 44:9-17)

The false prophet cannot tell the difference between a divine being and firewood. We are surrounded by these false prophets who deceive us into worshipping gods that cannot save. These gods claim to be our creators, kings, and rulers of culture. They are hoisted on shoulders and regularly paraded before us. The gods who are slowly seducing us to believe them are many, including

- the gods of advertising, who tell us that our happiness is packaged in a product;
- the gods of materialism, who tell us we are what we earn and own;
- the gods of fashion, who dictate our clothing budget;
- the gods of success, who teach us to manipulate each other;
- the gods of consumption, who strip the earth bare and leave nothing for our children;
- the gods of debt, who tell us we should have it now;
- the gods of alcohol and drugs, who numb us;
- the gods of sexual expression, who champion one-night stands over covenanted marriage bonds;
- the gods of politics, who make promises that can't be kept;
- the gods of power, who tell us we should never suffer;
- the gods of prestige, who crown TV idols and icons;
- the gods of sports, who rule our schedules more than a Christian calendar;
- the gods of fame, who invite us to be the next Survivor, American Idol, or Dancing Star.

These gods are everywhere! What do we do with them? Isaiah suggests that we laugh at them. The gods of our world have no life in them. We made them. We must carry them, fuss over them, protect them, defend them, and worship them. Our God is different. Our God carries us. His ways may surprise and startle us. His ways may be new. But his ways are saving.

Returning to the false prophet in Revelation 13, we find these words in verses 16-18:

> Also it causes all, both small and great, both rich and poor, both free and slave, to be marked on the right hand or the forehead, so that no one can buy or sell who does not have the mark, that is, the name of the beast or the number of its name. This calls for wisdom: let anyone with understanding calculate the number of the beast, for it is the number of a person. Its number is six hundred sixty-six.

So, we come to one of the popular speculations of the Revelation—666, the mark of the beast. The number is the name of a person. Theories abound about the mark of the beast. Somebody's saintly grandmother thought phone numbers were the mark of the beast. We got over that when Social Security numbers came out. Then it was credit card numbers and, after that, a computer in Brussels nicknamed the Beast (everybody's number was stored in its evil memory bank). The newest one is barcodes. Soon they'll be installing them on heads and hands so we can become our own credit cards. They will scan our eyes, heads, and hands at the checkout. They will debit our accounts on the spot. We'll be able to buy or sell with the mark of the barcode, but not without it.

I wonder if anybody ever thought about people in Calcutta who don't have phones, Social Security numbers, credit cards, or barcodes on their heads. It seems to me that a beast smart enough to deceive all the people on earth ought to be able to mark anybody anywhere without needing to depend on technology.

So what's the mark of the beast? What is 666? I'll give you my two best guesses.

1. The number 666 is the numerical name of Nero Caesar. Nero was a beastly emperor a few years before the writing of the Revelation. He was also rumored to be still living even though mortally wounded (remember the wound of the beast from the sea). People had not forgotten his cruelty to Christians. If you were going to choose a symbol of beastly power, Nero fit the bill. In John's day, they assigned numerical value to letters. This was true of Hebrew, Greek, and Latin. If you take the name NERO CAESAR in Hebrew and add it up, you get the following:

Nun	=	50
Resh	=	200
Vav	=	6
Qof	=	100
Samek	=	60
Resh	=	200
		616 Total

Oops! We're short by 50. But wait, some manuscripts of Revelation 13:18 actually read 616 instead of 666. This puzzled scholars for a long time. Then, among the Dead Sea Scrolls, Nero's name was found with a different spelling, NERON CAESAR. The extra Nun is worth 50. Voilà! 666!

Granted, this isn't nearly as fun as all the neat tricks you can do with the number 666. Did you know that when you take the name of Bill Gates III, convert it to the American Standard Code for Information Interchange (ASCII), and add all the numerical values, you get 666? Ronald Wilson Reagan has 6 numbers in each name, thus 666. Barney the Dinosaur can be numerically configured to become 666. John F. Kennedy received 666 votes at the 1956 Democratic Convention. This was all the reason many believers needed to oppose him for the presidency. Their beliefs were later confirmed when he died of a head wound.

Given all these theories, I cast my vote for bad old Nero, the beast who thought he was god, minted his image on coins, and called for worship across the empire. He died of a head wound and was superstitiously expected to make a comeback—kind of like Elvis. The cult kept the expectations alive.

2. The other possibility is that 666 is a 777 wannabe. Six is the number of futility and incompleteness. Seven is the perfect whole number. In the Revelation, there are seven churches, seven seals, seven angels blowing trumpets, seven bowls of wrath, seven blessings—well, you get the point. Six is always one short of seven. It can't quite do what it wants to do. Seven is God's fullness, power, and sovereignty. It is the number that finishes what it starts. So when John says 666, he is saying limited, on a leash, constrained, never able to fully conquer.

If we know that the sea beast is the emperor, and the land beast is the emperor cult, and 666 is old Nero, can we stop looking for these sinister beings out in the future? Yes and no.

Yes, we can stop adding up the numerical value of people's names. We can stop looking for someone, now alive, who will emerge as the leader of a unified world government and mark his followers. We can lay those nonbiblical ideas to rest.

But no, we can't stop looking for the beast that marks its followers. The beast lives on in any intimidator or deceiver who calls for our devotion, sacrifice, or worship. The beast is alive in every image of materialism, sexuality, or power that exalts itself above God. The beast marks it devotees on the head (in the way they think) and on the hand (the deeds they do). The beast lurks in charisma, religion, miracles, and images. The beast thrives in false advertising, sexual seduction, and get-rich schemes. The beast parades as fame, finesse, and fortune. The beast flaunts success, how-to, and winning. And this deceptive land beast who looks like a lamb and talks like a dragon can steal our lives.

Similar to the previous two stories of the Revelation (the sixth seal and the sixth trumpet), evil and destruction crescendo. Then comes a welcomed reprieve. Following the introduction of the two beasts, we are taken again into the presence of the Lamb.

> Then I looked, and there was the Lamb, standing on Mount Zion! And with him were one hundred forty-four thousand who had his name and his Father's name written on their foreheads. And I heard a voice from heaven like the sound of many waters and like the sound of loud thunder; the voice I heard was like the sound of harpists playing on their harps, and they sing a new song before the throne and before the four living creatures and before the elders.

No one could learn that song except the one hundred forty-four thousand who have been redeemed from the earth. (14:1-3)

This victory scene of the people of God ushers us into the presence of three angels who each make announcements. The first angel offers the gospel invitation: "Fear God and give him glory, for the hour of his judgment has come; and worship him who made heaven and earth, the sea and the springs of water" (v. 7). The second angel announces the fall of the great city: "Fallen, fallen is Babylon the great! She has made all nations drink of the wine of the wrath of her fornication" (v. 8). The third angel gives a warning:

Those who worship the beast and its image, and receive a mark on their foreheads or on their hands, they will also drink the wine of God's wrath, poured unmixed into the cup of his anger, and they will be tormented with fire and sulfur in the presence of the holy angels and in the presence of the Lamb. And the smoke of their torment goes up forever and ever. There is no rest day or night for those who worship the beast and its image and for anyone who receives the mark of its name. (Vv. 9-11)

Each angel clearly calls for uncompromised loyalty to the Lamb. They warn of the consequences of being seduced by the beasts. The clarion call to decisiveness is fittingly followed by two images of harvest—the wheat harvest by sickle and the grape harvest in the winepress of God's wrath. We'll reap what we sow.

As we reach the end of this tornado sighting, we do as we have done in the previous two narratives. We return to center stage, the throne room of God. There we see again the sea of glass. Twenty-six times in the Revelation we are told about the sea. It is an image of chaos. The Bible speaks about many seas. The unformed world of Genesis 1 is described as darkness hovering over the deep (v. 2). Noah's sea seemed to be the end of all living things. The Red Sea looked like a graveyard for God's people trying to exit Egypt. The churning, tossing sea prompted frightened disciples to interrupt Jesus's nap, asking, "Do you not care that we are perishing?" (Mark 4:38). The beast of Revelation 13 rises out of the sea. The sea holds the dead in its grip. All through the Bible the sea is viewed as a monster of chaos, ready to gobble us up, take us down, and swallow us whole. The chaotic sea is the world of the seven churches, ruled by Caesar. The chaotic sea is our world, where powers reduce and destroy us.

But in John's vision, there is hope in the middle of madness; there is a realm where evil is not sovereign. The sea in John's vision is like glass, without a wave or a ripple. It is quiet and still. The chaos is gone. At the end of the Revelation the sea is commanded to give up the dead in it. The beast and the dragon are tossed into the fiery lake. Then "a new heaven and a new earth" come down, "and the sea [is] no more" (Rev. 21:1).

Returning to the scene of the throne room and the sea of glass, we see the saints who have conquered the beast and its image, "standing beside the sea" (15:2). Singing "the song of Moses, the servant of God, and the song of the Lamb" (v. 3), they give voice to their praise:

Great and amazing are your deeds,
> Lord God the Almighty!
Just and true are your ways,
> King of the nations!

Lord, who will not fear
> and glorify your name?

For you alone are holy.
> All nations will come
> and worship before you,

for your judgments have been revealed. (Vv. 3-4)

The whirling tornado has spun a story about a woman and a child, a dragon and two beasts, a Lamb standing on Mount Zion with 144,000 faithful, and the harvest of the inhabitants of the earth. It feels like an ending, but it isn't. There is more to come. But we who are listening to what the Spirit says to the church are feeling more and more certain of the future and of the one in whose hand it lies.

Revelation 15–19: The Prostitute, the Funeral of a City, and the Banquet

The clue of what is to come next is contained in the final scene of our last vision as we are told that seven angels have seven plagues and that with these "the wrath of God is ended" (15:1, 5-8). Having seen the seven seals and the seven trumpets, and having been spared the seven thunders, which John is instructed not to write about (10:4), we have to imagine that the coming climax of judgment is the worst yet. And we would be correct.

The judgment is not complete because the dragon still yields his authority to the beast, who occupies earthly thrones. The false prophet supports the beast by deceiving the inhabitants of the earth and assimilating them into the cult of the empire. Until this is brought to an end, the judgment of God continues to shake the earth, in hopes of turning hearts from the beast to the Lamb.

The opening scene finds us in a tent-tabernacle similar to the meeting place of Moses and God. The thick smoke of glory tells us that we are in the rare air of holiness. Out of the tent come seven angels who have been given seven golden bowls full of the wrath of God. Earlier in the Revelation, these golden bowls contained the prayers of the saints for justice. Now these bowls contain the response of God to the evil inflicted upon the saints. The plagues contained in the bowls of wrath are reminiscent of the plagues poured out on Egypt—painful sores, water turned to blood, darkness over the land, frogs, and hail. "This clear link with Egypt," Peterson observes, "reinforces St. John's emphasis on worship, for . . . the ten plagues were not visited on the Egyptians because they were an extraordinarily evil people, but for a single reason which had no moral content to it at all: they were determined to keep Israel from worshipping God.[10]

As we walk through this vision in Revelation 15–19, note the references to worship that occur along the way. We will address worship as the Response of the People in the next chapter. Judgment is necessary as a shattering act of God to dislodge Pharaoh from stubborn resistance, thus granting people freedom to worship God. God will move heaven and earth to form a worshipping people.

The angels go forth from the tent of meeting to the world of resistance with golden bowls sloshing over with the wrath of God. The first angel pours painful, putrid sores upon those who worship and are

---

10. Peterson, *Reversed Thunder*, 143.

marked by the beast. The second angel pours wrath upon the sea, and it turns to deadly blood. The third angel pours his bowl into the rivers and streams, and they also turn to blood. Koester observes that rather than the biblical punishment that demands a life for a life from those who shed blood, the justice meted out here, although poetic in form, only demands that the blood shedders drink from waters contaminated with blood. Clearly the intention is not so much punishment as it is to bring about repentance.[11]

The fourth angel pours his bowl of wrath on the sun, and it is allowed to scorch the people of the earth with fire. Given the divine intent to turn people to repentance, we are told that "they cursed the name of God, who had authority over these plagues, and they did not repent and give him glory" (16:9). They demonstrate that loyalty to evil is hard core, deep in the human heart. Imagine the seven churches having heard the series of judgments, knowing that some within the congregations are quasi-loyal to the cult of the empire and its economic privilege and that others have been lulled into complacency by the comforts of the empire. The stakes are becoming clear—worship the beast or worship the Lamb. Nothing in between will escape the judgment of God.

> **Judgment is necessary as a shattering act of God to dislodge Pharaoh from stubborn resistance, thus granting people freedom to worship God. God will move heaven and earth to form a worshipping people.**

Like the transition from number four to number five in the other visions, we move from similar plagues in numbers one through four to

---

11. Koester, *Revelation and the End*, 149–50.

ministories in numbers five through seven. When the fifth angel pours his bowl of wrath over the throne of the beast, the kingdom of the beast is cast into darkness. We are reminded of the darkness in Egypt that enveloped those with privileged power (Exod. 10:21).

The sixth angel pours his bowl of wrath into the Euphrates River, a protective barrier to the east for the Roman Empire. The drying up of the river makes Rome vulnerable to its enemies. In response, the evil trinity burps frogs from its mouth that go into the world to gather the kings of the earth. They gather in defense of any attack from the east. The place of this military assemblage is called Armageddon (from Hebrew: *Har* [meaning "mountain"] + *Megiddo* [the plain in northern Israel] = Ar-mageddon). This is an Old Testament site of numerous battles where the enemies of the people of God are defeated. The frog-gathered military coalition is not in for a good outcome.

The seventh and final bowl of wrath is poured into the air. The scene that erupts is similar to the concluding barrage of a massive fireworks display. It is bigger, louder, and more explosive than anything we have seen yet:

> And there came flashes of lightning, rumblings, peals of thunder, and a violent earthquake, such as had not occurred since people were upon the earth, so violent was that earthquake.... And every island fled away, and no mountains were to be found; and huge hailstones, each weighing about a hundred pounds, dropped from heaven on people, until they cursed God for the plague of the hail, so fearful was that plague. (Rev. 16:18, 20)

The benediction of the bowls of wrath is stated with the declaration, "It is done!" (v. 17). We are given to understand that "it" is the fall of the great city Babylon. The wine cup of the fury of God's wrath is poured out on her. This is the story we are to hear next.

For many readers of the Revelation, the story of the great prostitute-harlot-whore in chapters 17–19 is the definitive message of the Apocalypse. Without question, the prostitute is Rome, the city on seven hills that stands as the center of military and economic power for the world. It is important that we understand what this symbol of the prostitute means to the people of the seven churches and to us. Eugene Peterson helps us. He explains that apocalyptic literature uses exaggeration to clarify those "mysterious powers" in our lives that get "distorted through the smudged window glass of our culture." Concerning the great prostitute, he observes that in our daily lives we experience it as a very pleasant, livable city. But by seeing the city caricatured as a great prostitute, we are made unforgettably aware of "the powerfully seductive presence of those who would obstruct or subvert our worship of the slain and risen Lamb."[12]

The constant seduction of the world's principalities and powers is a continuous drip, drip, drip pressure on us to compromise. The temptation to follow in the way of the empire is relentless. Only a healthy eschatology (understanding of God's future) can give the soul the ballast needed to withstand the assimilating pressures from every side. John gifts us with an effective image-story that details the

---

12. Peterson, *Reversed Thunder*, 145-46.

consequences awaiting people who cave to the empire. He reaches his descriptive genius in Revelation 17–19.[13]

He stages a drama for an audience consisting of two groups—those who served the beast and those who braved the beast by faithfulness to the Lamb. His drama reminds me of the Carousel of Progress at Walt Disney World, Florida. It is an exhibit that observes a family during three stages of their electric life: past, present, and future. It shows how far we've come and where we're headed with household technology and gadgets.

I think John's story might be called the Carousel of Destruction. In three acts, John shows the future of the prostitute and her followers.

Act I

The Great Prostitute

> Then one of the seven angels who had the seven bowls came and said to me, "Come, I will show you the judgment of the great whore who is seated on many waters, with whom the kings of the earth have committed fornication, and with the wine of whose fornication the inhabitants of the earth have become drunk." So he carried me away in the spirit into a wilderness, and I saw a woman sitting on a scarlet beast that was full of blasphemous names, and it had seven heads and ten horns. The woman was clothed in purple and scarlet, and adorned with gold and jewels and pearls, holding in her hand a golden cup full of abominations and the impurities of her fornication; and on her forehead was written a name, a mystery: "Babylon the great, mother of whores and of earth's

---

13. The following is adapted and expanded from my earlier book on the Revelation, *Answers for Chicken Little* (Kansas City: Beacon Hill Press of Kansas City, 2005), 98-107.

abominations." And I saw that the woman was drunk with the blood of the saints and the blood of the witnesses to Jesus. When I saw her, I was greatly amazed. (17:1-6)

The great prostitute is impressive. She looks as if she just walked out of Saks Fifth Avenue, dressed in purple and scarlet, the finest threads of the day. This lady is no Walmart shopper. She wears gold, pearls, and gemstones. She is sassy. She is the mother of all prostitutes. Her limousine is a beast. She rides sidesaddle, tipsy from drinking the polluted filth of the sewer and the blood of martyred saints. She is arrogant, smooth, wealthy, powerful, cultured, and luxurious. She has everything she wants, and she flaunts it.

While this description is seductive in many ways, it is also a caricature of other depictions of Rome. These other images are less drunk and saucy, more controlled and controlling. While some are allured by this image, others snicker at this lady of the night.

Her clientele is impressive—kings, merchants, shipping magnates (18:9-19). The leaders of the world are listed in her little black book. The barons of Wall Street, the smug power brokers of the old money clubs, the entrepreneurs of note, the world's wealthiest—all are her clients. They have given up and given in to her ways in order to taste the good life of the empire. They have staked their lives on her ability to satisfy them. She is their hope.

And John says, "When I saw her, I was greatly amazed" (17:6). You would be too. Evil rarely looks ugly when we first see it. Rome is an elegantly seductive prostitute, impressive enough to catch John's eye. Introduce a dirty old street woman with wrinkled skin and matted hair, and we wouldn't take a second glance. The dark side always puts its best foot forward, hooking our desires and reeling us in.

The carousel is moving. Hold on.

Act II

The Pimp

In one of my pastorates, I learned a lot about prostitution. Seductively dressed women walked the street in front of our church. Sometimes they would come in for water or to use the restroom or to get warm. Each prostitute is only the tip of the iceberg. Behind her is a powerful pimp, the enforcer who protects her turf and sees to it that all the clients pay. Evil is never free. The pimp furnishes the prostitute with lies, luxury, and legal services. He pumps her ego, disguises her body, and uses her for his profit.

Rome had a pimp, the best in the business.

The angel said to me, "Why are you so amazed? I will tell you the mystery of the woman, and of the beast with seven heads and ten horns that carries her. The beast that you saw was, and is not, and is about to ascend from the bottomless pit and go to destruction. And the inhabitants of the earth, whose names have not been written in the book of life from the foundation of the world, will be amazed when they see the beast, because it was and is not and is to come." (17:7-8)

We have seen this pimp before in the Revelation. This is the beast summoned by Satan out of the sea in chapter 13. This beast is a parody of the Lamb and even bears the title "it was and is not and is to come." We are reminded of the one we met earlier in Revelation 1 "who is and who was and who is to come" (v. 4). This beast wants to be as permanent as the Lamb but is on a restricted time leash.

Satan and the beast have had other prostitutes before—Egypt and Babylon, to name a couple of famous ones. He used them up and left them in ruins. (You can read about the demise of Egypt in Exod. 12:29–14:30 and about Babylon in Isa. 46–47.) Now the pimp has Rome.

One day, one of our city prostitutes came to my church office to tell me she wanted out. She was tired of selling herself. When I suggested that she just quit, fear seized her. "He'll kill me. He's already broken girls' arms and noses. Nobody quits." I called a church five hundred miles away and arranged for them to meet her at the bus station. She left to pack her things and say goodbye to a few friends. She was to meet me back at the church, and we would go to the bus station. She never showed. I never saw her again. I've often wondered if her pimp got wind of her plans.

In John's drama, the pimp turns on the prostitute and devours her. Why? She got into a fight with a Lamb and lost. She's used up. What good is she anymore? The clear connection between the prostitute and Rome is noted in the following verses. The seven churches would readily understand this to be in reference to the geography and emperors of Rome, past, present, and future.

"This calls for a mind that has wisdom: the seven heads are seven mountains on which the woman is seated; also, they are seven kings, of whom five have fallen, one is living, and the other has not yet come; and when he comes, he must remain only a little while. As for the beast that was and is not, it is an eighth but it belongs to the seven, and it goes to destruction. And the ten horns that you saw are ten kings who have not yet received a kingdom, but they are to receive authority as kings for one hour, together with the beast. These are united in yielding their power and authority to the beast; they will make war on the Lamb, and the Lamb will conquer them, for he is Lord of lords and King of kings, and those with him are called and chosen and faithful."

And he said to me, "The waters that you saw, where the whore is seated, are peoples and multitudes and nations and languages. And the ten horns that you saw, they and the beast will hate the whore; they will make her desolate and naked; they will devour her flesh and burn her up with fire. For God has put it into their hearts to carry out his purpose by agreeing to give their kingdom to the beast, until the words of God will be fulfilled. The woman you saw is the great city that rules over the kings of the earth." (Rev. 17:9-18)

In the end, evil devours itself. It can do no other. It has no capacity to create, birth new life, heal, or restore. It can only seduce, destroy, and kill. The very prostitute that yielded her being to the beast is now stripped naked, devoured, and incinerated by the same power that pumped her ego full of arrogance. Evil turns on its own; it destroys its carriers. Evil uses and discards. And God allows it to happen. Evil is a six, not a seven. It is incomplete. It remains unfulfilled. It cannot finish what it starts. God stands in the way. So evil unleashes its fury on itself.

A cosmic death has occurred. Let the funeral begin:

After this I saw another angel coming down from heaven, having great authority; and the earth was made bright with his splendor. He called out with a mighty voice,

> "Fallen, fallen is Babylon the great!
>> It has become a dwelling place of demons,
> a haunt of every foul spirit,
>> a haunt of every foul bird,
>> a haunt of every foul and hateful beast.
> For all the nations have drunk
>> of the wine of the wrath of her fornication,
> and the kings of the earth have committed fornication with her,
>> and the merchants of the earth have grown rich from the power of her luxury."

Then I heard another voice from heaven saying,

> "Come out of her, my people,
>> so that you do not take part in her sins,
> and so that you do not share in her plagues;
> for her sins are heaped high as heaven,
>> and God has remembered her iniquities.
> Render to her as she herself has rendered,
>> and repay her double for her deeds;
>> mix a double draught for her in the cup she mixed.
> As she glorified herself and lived luxuriously,
>> so give her a like measure of torment and grief.

> Since in her heart she says,
>> 'I rule as a queen;
> I am no widow,
>> and I will never see grief,'
> therefore her plagues will come in a single day—
>> pestilence and mourning and famine—
> and she will be burned with fire;
>> for mighty is the Lord God who judges her." (18:1-8)

This is the announcement of the prostitute's demise. Rome, once powerful, seductive, and mesmerizing, is now a buzzard-infested place of doom, decay, and demons. The enticement is gone. Evil comes to an end. It is a ruined civilization with worn-out ideas, failed philosophies, and empty lifestyles. Rubble lies where the glorious city once stood. The prostitute cannot defeat the Lamb, because in her dying, the Lamb exposes the prostitute as a carrier of death. The collapse is catastrophic.

However, in the middle of the funeral, God interjects a timeless invitation to all who have lived under the power of the empire. "Come out of her, my people, so that you do not take part in her sins, and so that you do not share in her plagues" (v. 4). Grace is offered to the clients of the prostitute. They are the beloved creatures of God whose lives have been reduced and cheapened by the seduction of the prostitute. We see amazing grace in the midst of ruin.

The carousel is moving again.

Act III
The Clients in the Little Black Book

The final scene lists the devastated clients, those whose names were found in the prostitute's little black book. Kings, CEOs, politicians, real estate agents, merchants, grocers, car dealers, department store managers, clerks, hair stylists, advertising agents, athletes, pastors, military personnel, truckers, computer programmers, teachers, scientists—well, that would be the list if John were writing to our century.

Their world has crashed. It has gone up in smoke. The devastated clients stand before the ruins and say,

> "Alas, alas, the great city,
> Babylon, the mighty city!
> For in one hour your judgment has come."

And the merchants of the earth weep and mourn for her, since no one buys their cargo anymore, cargo of gold, silver, jewels and pearls, fine linen, purple, silk and scarlet, all kinds of scented wood, all articles of ivory, all articles of costly wood, bronze, iron, and marble, cinnamon, spice, incense, myrrh, frankincense, wine, olive oil, choice flour and wheat, cattle and sheep, horses and chariots, slaves—and human lives.

> "The fruit for which your soul longed
> has gone from you,
> and all your dainties and your splendor
> are lost to you,
> never to be found again!"

The merchants of these wares, who gained wealth from her, will stand far off, in fear of her torment, weeping and mourning aloud,

> "Alas, alas, the great city,
> clothed in fine linen,
> in purple and scarlet,
> adorned with gold,

> with jewels, and with pearls!
>
> For in one hour all this wealth has been laid waste!"
>
> And all shipmasters and seafarers, sailors and all whose trade is on the sea, stood far off and cried out as they saw the smoke of her burning,
>
> "What city was like the great city?"
>
> And they threw dust on their heads, as they wept and mourned, crying out,
>
> "Alas, alas, the great city,
>> where all who had ships at sea
>> grew rich by her wealth!
>
> For in one hour she has been laid waste." (Rev. 18:10-19)

They mourn, wail, grieve, and throw dust on their heads. They say, "Alas, alas." I don't remember the last time I heard someone say "Alas, alas," but I do remember the last time I heard someone cuss. I think "Alas, alas" was about the same as cussing back then.

I've started listening carefully to people who curse. I think they are saying more than they realize. Life is not turning out as they had hoped. The powers in whom they deposited their hopes have let them down. Their dreams have been laid to waste. Loneliness, torment, and futility fill the dark holes in their hearts. They have been used instead of loved. They have been trashed instead of treasured. Often their curses are aimed at God, similar to the inhabitants of the earth in Revelation 16:9, 21. When they use the name of Jesus Christ as a curse, they are identifying the Lamb who defeated their prostitute and brought their petty empire to an end. They know that they are damned by their chosen loyalty. So they curse as a confession of the consequence.

Act III ends with a soliloquy of emptiness:

With such violence Babylon the great city
> will be thrown down,
> and will be found no more;

and the sound of harpists and minstrels and of flutists and trumpeters
> will be heard in you no more;

and an artisan of any trade
> will be found in you no more;

and the sound of the millstone
> will be heard in you no more;

and the light of a lamp
> will shine in you no more;

and the voice of bridegroom and bride
> will be heard in you no more;

for your merchants were the magnates of the earth,
> and all nations were deceived by your sorcery.

And in you was found the blood of prophets and of saints,
> and of all who have been slaughtered on earth. (18:21-24)

The Carousel of Destruction in three acts grinds to a halt. The show is over. The funeral is ended. The final word has been said. Or has it? We find that our carousel is moving again. Can there be another act?

Yes. We are greeted by a multitude in heaven as they announce,
> "Hallelujah!

> Salvation and glory and power to our God,
>> for his judgments are true and just;
> he has judged the great whore
>> who corrupted the earth with her fornication,
> and he has avenged on her the blood of his servants." . . .

And the twenty-four elders and the four living creatures fell down and worshiped God who is seated on the throne, saying,

> "Amen. Hallelujah!"

And from the throne came a voice saying,

> "Praise our God,
>> all you his servants,
>> and all who fear him,
> small and great."

Then I heard what seemed to be the voice of a great multitude, like the sound of many waters and like the sound of mighty thunderpeals, crying out,

> "Hallelujah!
> For the Lord our God
>> the Almighty reigns.
> Let us rejoice and exult
>> and give him the glory,
> for the marriage of the Lamb has come,
>> and his bride has made herself ready;
> to her it has been granted to be clothed
>> with fine linen, bright and pure"—

for the fine linen is the righteous deeds of the saints. (19:1-2, 4-8)

We know these people. They have remained true to the Lamb, suffered under the beast, given faithful witness in the streets of the great city, cried out from beneath the altar of God for justice, and sung the praise of God at the throne. They have not compromised for convenience, been assimilated by seduction, or grown cold in lethargy. And they are called the bride of the Lamb.

The Lamb has a bride, a beautiful bride. Her beauty doesn't come from the powder and plastic of a prostitute, but from the grace in her lover's eyes. Her attraction is not lustful seduction, but vibrant life. Her master is not a powerful beast, but a risen Lord. Her destiny is not ruin, but a banquet. Her clothes are not cheap and racy, but pure and white. Her devotion is not to all paying customers, but to the one who laid down his life in loving sacrifice.

Both images—prostitute and bride—are about the same intimate relationship. But the outcomes could not be more telling. As Eugene Peterson observes, for the prostitute, sex becomes a matter of commerce, contract, and calculation. But for the bride, sex is about love, relational commitment, and self-giving. Thus in Revelation 18 we find the lament of merchants and sea traders for the downfall of the great prostitute, because their money-driven, self-indulgent, self-centered religion has come to ruin. Left with themselves, these worshippers of the great prostitute are lost. By contrast, Revelation displays many images of those belonging to the bride who give of themselves, worshipping, praising, and serving God. For them,

> The Lamb has a bride, a beautiful bride. Her beauty doesn't come from the powder and plastic of a prostitute, but from the grace in her lover's eyes.

worship is about continuous self-giving trust and loving commitment; it is not a contract for commercial profit and immediate self-gratification. The former is about the truth that leads to life; the latter, a lie that leads to emptiness and death.[14]

The story of Revelation 17–19 moves from the pits of Bad News to the heights of Good News. And for all who read the Revelation as fodder for futuristic speculation, please pause to realize that the Apocalypse is about our identity as humans, our devotion to our creator, our worship of the Lamb who loves us, and the call to a life of holy love. The literature may be strange, but the gospel of the redeeming God flows from the heart of the narrative.

Revelation 19–22: The Termination of Evil, Final Judgment, the New Jerusalem

We concluded the last vision with the news that Babylon, the great city depicted as a prostitute, has fallen. Following her funeral, we are treated to a wedding rehearsal and told that the bride has made herself ready. We are poised for a walk down the aisle. But similar to the other visions, every time we settle down before the throne of God and grow accustomed to hearing praise, we get whisked away into the throes of judgment and battle. The tornado has set down in another Bad News neighborhood and is spinning another story.

This time the story will take us to the end, which we will discover to be our new beginning. The vision we are given in Revelation 19:11-21 recognizes that though the prostitute is gone and Babylon is fallen,

---

14. Peterson, *Reversed Thunder*, 146-48.

the evil trinity that empowered her is still on the loose. The one who will resolve this opposition is introduced in verses 11-16.

"Faithful and True" rides a white horse (v. 11). His eyes are like fire, he wears many crowns, and his robe is dipped in his own sacrificial blood. He is called "The Word of God" (v. 13), his only weapon is a sharp sword that proceeds from his mouth, and the inscription on his robe and thigh is "King of kings and Lord of lords" (v. 16). Though we are given his names, we are also told that he has a secret name that only he knows. His power is unknown to anyone else. No one can utter this name as a way of evoking his power for their purposes. We are also told that he will rule the nations with a rod of iron.

Unquestionably, we are seeing the Son of Man, the slaughtered Lamb at the throne, the child attacked by the dragon in Revelation 12, the victor over the prostitute in Revelation 17, and the groom of the bride in Revelation 19. John's vision collects the images of Jesus and amasses them in one final conquering portrait in this last vision. While many are averse to depicting God with warlike images, note that there is only one weapon present in the scene that follows—the Word of God. Just as the saints in battle with the dragon (12:11) overcame "by the blood of the Lamb" and "the word of their testimony," the Lamb on the white horse bears bloodstains and fights evil with the Word of God. While the white-robed armies of heaven accompany him on their white horses, they do nothing to achieve the victory. The Lamb has all the power needed.

The battle scene (19:17-21) takes us back to an earlier vision where the beast and the false prophet gather the kings of the earth at Armageddon (16:12-16). This historic Old Testament battleground, the site of opposition to the people of God, is to be the waterloo of the beast and the false prophet. Even before the battle commences, an angel sends a banquet invitation to the birds and buzzards. They are invited to feast on flesh on the field of Armageddon (19:17).

The action is swift and decisive. The beast and the false prophet are captured and thrown alive into the lake of fire that burns with sulfur (v. 20). The rest, the kings of the earth gathered in opposition to the Lamb, are slain by the word of his mouth and become buzzard food. The contrasts of the Revelation are intentional. Having just seen the wedding supper of the Lamb, we now see the buzzard banquet of evil, where the opposition is the main course. The dualism of apocalyptic literature gives us paired polar opposites throughout the narratives: the Holy Trinity and the evil trinity, the Lamb who is and the beast who isn't, the seductive prostitute and the pure bride, the foul city of Babylon and the new Jerusalem, the words that are false and the words that are true. While the images and symbols come and go in the stories, their counterparts are always in the back of our minds.

With the beast and the false prophet gone, Revelation 20:1-10 turns to Satan, the old accusing devil. An angel with the key to the bottomless pit comes from heaven, seizes the old dragon, binds him, and throws him into the pit for a thousand years. After the thousand years, he must be let out for a little while. Following this, the martyred saints are resurrected to reign with Christ for an equal thousand years. They serve as priests during this reign.

This is ground zero for the clash of millennial theories: premillennialism, postmillennialism, and amillennialism. Rather than reviewing these theories of the end-time, I would suggest that the thousand years are not meant to be placed on a calendar. Just as Armageddon is not meant to be located on a geography map, this thousand-year period is not meant to suggest a future period during which Satan is bound. We discredit the nature of apocalyptic when we take symbols and interpret them literally rather than grasping what they mean. The thousand-year period refers to fullness, and the reign of the saints suggests that evil can be overcome. Jesus spoke in the Gospels of the binding of the strong man. Even before the final demise of the devil, there is a power at work among the priests of God that is effective. Our victories over evil in this present time are real, and they suggest the coming moment when evil itself will be no more.

Satan is released from the pit and makes one final desperate effort to reclaim creation. He appears the last time to deceive the nations of the earth. He calls for one named Gog from the land of Magog (a reference to Ezek. 38–39) to assist him in amassing an army (Rev. 20:8). This massive army surrounds the encampment of the saints and their beloved city. But before any attack can be launched, fire falls from heaven and consumes them all. The devil is thrown into the lake of fire, where the beast and the false prophet await him, and they are tormented forever and ever. We are done with the evil trinity.

Many find these bloody, lake-of-fire, eternal-torment texts of the Revelation offensive to their senses—and rightly so. Having seen in the story of Jesus the mercy and compassion of God, vindictive punishment seems unbecoming. It is important that we remember that the Revelation is not written to celebrate the demise of the inhabitants of the earth who worshipped the beast. It is written to awaken people to the consequences of such a choice. The focal point of these visions is the impact they are having on the congregants gathered in seven cities on the Lord's Day, listening to the visions given to John. The purpose of the Revelation is a call to repentance and an encouragement to live faithfully.

Many who embrace pacifism and oppose war, find these battle scenes difficult to swallow. We rarely sing the old staple of past vacation Bible schools: "Onward Christian soldiers! Marching as to war."[15] We have gotten much tamer, much nicer. My work has occasioned me to have many friends in The Salvation Army. They embrace an identity that has war as a guiding image. They know they are up against forces that dehumanize their fellow humans, and they intend to invade the enemy territory and offer grace in the streets of Babylon. I find their courage and sacrifice refreshingly like the Apocalypse saints.

Eugene Peterson points out that salvation draws us into a war against an enemy, a war in which victory has already been won through the cross of Christ, but a war nevertheless. The war portrayed in the Revelation is intended to call us to battle against opposing forces by obediently living out our salvation to its fullest extent.[16] Perhaps we have become too complacent with the evil that surrounds us. Perhaps the apocalypse is doing its work on us—calling us to be vigilant in the battle of the Lamb. We have much to learn from the Revelation.

On the heels of this final judgment of the evil trinity, we see a great white throne so impressive that earth and heaven flee from its presence.

---

15. Sabine Baring-Gould, "Onward, Christian Soldiers," in *Sing to the Lord*, no. 644.
16. Peterson, *Reversed Thunder*, 160-61.

All the dead, great and small, are raised for the final judgment, and the books are opened—the book of life, which contains the names of the people of God, and the book of works, which records the deeds of each person. Once death and the grave have offered up their dead, they are thrown into the lake of fire. Don't miss this. God extinguishes death and the grave in the final judgment. They have had their last say and are no more. The chilling summary of the judgment is 20:15, "And anyone whose name was not found written in the book of life was thrown into the lake of fire."

The revelation of the Revelation is that we are pursued by the Lamb of God, offered salvation, invited to worship before the throne, called out of Babylon, and empowered to withstand the beast and his seduction. What we do with this reality matters. We will give account for how we respond to our creator and the one who died for us. We are shown the consequences of opposition to the ways of God. And the immediate function of the Revelation, as it is being read to the seven churches, is that the people who hear it will obey what they hear, come out of Babylon, and be encouraged in their present resistance to the beast.

> The revelation of the Revelation is that we are pursued by the Lamb of God, offered salvation, invited to worship before the throne, called out of Babylon, and empowered to withstand the beast and his seduction.

Some have suggested that mention of the names written in the book of life *from the foundation of the world* supports a theory of predestination—that is, some are predestined to be saved, and others are predestined to be lost. This would go against the grain of everything we have heard in the Revelation. Every person, every inhabitant of the earth, every tribe, every language, and every nation is invited into the salvation of the Lamb. The invitation is clear: "Let everyone who is thirsty come. Let anyone who wishes take the water of life as a gift" (22:17). The book of life is open for additions. The grace of God is for all who believe. Who we choose to worship and obey matters eternally.

The Bad News is over. The Good News now cascades in visions of a world without prostitute, Babylon, empire, devil, dragon, beast, or false prophet. All have exited through the bottom of the stage. We are left with new scenery right out of the rafters of heaven itself. Chapter 21 introduces a new heaven and a new earth, and the sea is no more. The primal sea of dark chaos is gone. The organ plays the opening score of "Here Comes the Bride." We see the new Jerusalem, the holy city, "coming down out of heaven from God, . . . as a bride adorned for her husband" (v. 2). Babylon is gone; the new Jerusalem is here. The prostitute is gone; the bride is here. The old is gone; the new is here. The foul is gone; the holy is here. The devil is gone; God is here.

This scene corrects much that is wrong with our folk theology. The earth is not destroyed; it is made new. This is our Father's world. He will not abandon it. We do not escape earth for heaven, but rather God removes the barrier that separates earth and heaven and they become one. The Lord's Prayer is fully and finally answered. God's will is done on earth even as it is done in heaven. Rapture does not take us up to God, but God comes down to us. The grand announcement is made:

See, the home of God is among mortals.

He will dwell with them;

they will be his peoples,

and God himself will be with them;

he will wipe every tear from their eyes.

Death will be no more;

mourning and crying and pain will be no more,

for the first things have passed away. (Vv. 3-4)

And finally, we hear the voice of the one seated on the throne as he says, "See, I am making all things new" (v. 5). It does not say that God will make *all new things* but rather that God makes *all things new*. God will take what is already in existence and restore it. God will redeem his creation, not trash it and start over again.

John is addressed next. This exchange is something of a bookend reference. The same titles used in the opening greeting are used again in the last vision (21:6). We were introduced in Revelation 1 to the one "who is and who was and who is to come" (vv. 4, 8), "the Alpha and the Omega" (v. 8), and "the first and the last" (v. 17). These time references are rooted in the name Yahweh, the name given to Moses (see Exod. 3:13-14). "Yahweh" is the conjugation of the verb "to be" ("is," "was," "will be"). The name speaks of presence in time. We hear in Revelation 22 the same titles again: "See, I am coming soon; my reward is with me, to repay according to everyone's work. I am the Alpha and the Omega, the first and the last, the beginning and the end" (vv. 12-13).

Returning to chapter 21, the timeless one issues the invitation, "To the thirsty I will give water as a gift from the spring of the water of life" (v. 6). It remains imperative that we drink of this life-gift-water because only those who drink will be citizens of the new Jerusalem.

Beast behavior will not be found in the city: "The cowardly, the faithless, the polluted, the murderers, the fornicators, the sorcerers, the idolaters, and all liars" will not be found in the city, but in the lake of fire (v. 8). These are the very behaviors that have already been confronted in the letters to the seven churches. This is the way of the beast.

Finally, here comes the bride. "Then one of the seven angels who had the seven bowls full of the seven last plagues came and said to me, 'Come, I will show you the bride, the wife of the Lamb.' And in the spirit he carried me away to a great, high mountain and showed me the holy city Jerusalem coming down out of heaven from God" (vv. 9-10). The city is a symmetrical cube, covering fifteen hundred square miles (roughly the equivalent of the Roman Empire on the ground, but also extending the same height into the heavens). This is also a thousand times larger than Ezekiel's restored Jerusalem in Ezekiel 40–47. The glory of God is described with jewels reflecting light. The wall of the city has twelve gates, three on each side, attended by angels. They are inscribed with the names of the twelve tribes of Israel. The wall of the city has twelve foundations, each adorned with a rare jewel, inscribed with the names of the apostles of the Lamb. The twelve gates are each a single pearl, and the streets are paved with gold. Compare this splendid city of the bride with the funeral dirge of Babylon in Revelation 18. You see the difference between the reward of the Lamb and the reward of the beast.

Given the significant references to the temple throughout the Revelation, we are expecting to hear about the temple in the city. For ancient Jerusalem, the temple on Mount Zion was the centerpiece of the city. Here however,

> I saw no temple in the city, for its temple is the Lord God the Almighty and the Lamb. And the city has no need of sun or moon to shine on it, for the glory of God is its light, and its lamp is the Lamb. The nations will walk by its light, and the kings of the earth will bring their glory into it. Its gates will never be shut by day—and there will be no night there. People will bring into it the glory and the honor of the nations. But nothing unclean will enter it, nor anyone who practices abomination or falsehood, but only those who are written in the Lamb's book of life. (21:22-27)

The temple has always been about the presence of God among the people. From the early traveling tabernacle of the wilderness to the ornate temple of Jerusalem, God has not desired a building but rather a presence where worship occurs. There were barriers to access (inner and outer courtyards) in the earthly temple, but here we find that the gates of the holy city are always open.

We have been accustomed to seeing the kings of the earth as enemies of the Lamb because so many of them sided with the beast throughout the Apocalypse. Here, however, we see the kings of the earth bringing "their glory" (their economies, art, labor and skill, systems of justice, diversity, and contributions to human thriving) into the city (v. 24). God is not antiking, anticity, or antination. Under the worship of the Lamb, these are welcomed.

It is the desire of God to heal the very nations that the beast has destroyed:

> Then the angel showed me the river of the water of life, bright as crystal, flowing from the throne of God and of the Lamb through the middle of the street of the city. On either side of the river is the tree of life with its twelve kinds of fruit, producing its fruit each month; and the leaves of the tree are for the healing of the nations. Nothing accursed will be found there anymore. But the throne of God and of the Lamb will be in it, and his servants will worship him; they will see his face, and his name will be on their foreheads. And there will be no more night; they need no light of lamp or sun, for the Lord God will be their light, and they will reign forever and ever. (22:1-5)

The thriving life of the garden of Eden, with capacity for two, is now found in the fifteen-hundred-square-mile city for everyone. The multiple trees of life bear constant fruit and are for the healing of the nations. Eating from the tree is no longer forbidden. It is offered to all who come bearing the name of the Lamb.

This is not just the end of our Apocalypse but also the end of our biblical canon of books. From the creation and fall of humankind in Genesis to the final redemption of the earth in the Revelation, we have journeyed in a story that we are still living. And from the sound of Revelation 22, this is not our ending; it is our new beginning. In this city, we dwell as diverse peoples, the nations are healed, we bring our crafts into the city as expressions that glorify God, and we worship the Lamb. This does not sound like an escape from earth but rather the fulfillment of God's intent for earth and heaven. This sounds like the beginning of a story that has no Bad News, no evil trinity, no seductive life-draining empires, and no darkness. Humans can thrive here! This is not an escape from anything, but the completion of everything.

The epilogue reminds us to worship only this God, to protect the integrity of the prophecy by not adding to or subtracting from it, and to extend the grand invitation to all who are thirsty. We will revisit the benediction in the final chapter.

Prayer

Gracious God, your judgment is so fierce that we
possess no confidence to face it in ourselves.
The earth trembles before your holiness.
But you have come to us as one of us in Jesus.
You have bridged the gap between our sin and your holiness.
Jesus has become as one of us that we might be made like you.
It is only by your grace that we have hope of
salvation. Thank you for such love.
We are unworthy of it, but deeply grateful to
be included in your global family.
Help us to live in the awareness that other gods,
other powers, other devils, would seduce us,
but only you can redeem us.
Make us the people you intended that we be—
worshippers of the Lamb, witnesses to the life that is truly life.
Amen.

5

The Response of the People

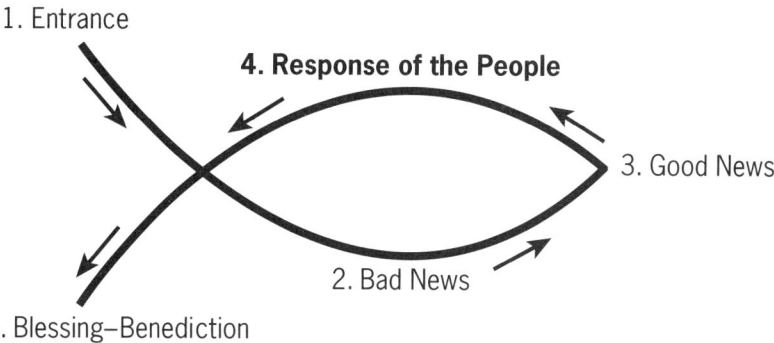

I have suggested that the plot of stories is also the plot of our gatherings for worship. Our lives spin in and out of worship on a seven-day cycle. Similar to the movement of a tornado (minus the destruction), we touch down once every seven days and are enmeshed in a radical whirling story that redefines the next six days. In the sanctuary of God, among the people of God, under the telling of the good news, we are turned right side up for life in an upside-down world.

The flow of worship is as follows:

- We are given *Entrance* to the presence of the Holy God, the one who sits on the throne, the Alpha and Omega, the first and the last, the Lamb, the seven spirits that proceed from God into the world. We sing the praise of this God as a reminder of where we are and in whose presence we are.

- Then we confess the distance and separation between a God like this and a world like ours. We admit the *Bad News* that our world is broken, we are compromised, evil is pervasive, and the inhabitants of the world are enslaved. This brutal honesty flies in the face of the empire's insistence that Caesar is on the throne and all is right in the world. Our confession is political treason. We declare that the emperor has no clothes, his bank account is empty, his ways are violent, and his power enslaving. Only in the context of honesty before the throne of God is worship authentic. But we do not stop at the confession of the Bad News.

- We declare the *Good News* that the judgment of God has fallen on Babylon. This stern mercy of God opens seeing eyes and hearing ears to a message of repentance. But judgment is not the only Good News. The Lamb has come among us in suffering love as conqueror, comforter, and counselor. He is our way, truth, and life. We are not alone. The Good News also includes a new perspective from the throne of God that enables us to see our present world through a different lens and thus interpret it in a different way. We are claimed as a people by God, given identity and mission in the world. Finally, we are infused with hope as we imagine the intrusion of the new Jerusalem into our old Babylon. We see what it looks like for the will of God to be done on earth, even as it is in heaven. We imagine and realize

the kingdoms of this world as the kingdom of our God and of his Christ.
- Having heard this Good News, we are now emboldened to offer the *Response of the People*. We are more than assenters who listen to the Bad News, Good News story and nod approval. We are disciples of the Lamb with work to do in the world. Our response includes worship, witness, testimony, resistance, vocation, urgency, and costly nonparticipation in the ways of Babylon. Even as we are still gathered in worship, we begin to plant the seeds of obedience in our songs, prayers, and practices.
- Finally, we are *Blessed* and sent into the world as the missional people of God, made like our God, living the way of the Lamb, committed to live faithfully in the streets of Babylon.

The weekly repetition of this story slowly forms us as a people who are living out an alternative script. It is interesting that the visions of the Revelation are told in sevens. Six of the seven parts of a vision occur in the world, and as we approach the seventh part, we return to the throne of God for a fresh perspective. Corporate worship follows the same pattern. After six days in the world, we gather corporately at the throne to have our imagination renewed. Worship is the habitual submission of our lives to the story of God.

Worship as a Response of the People

Given the politically charged context of the world of the seven churches, it is important to note that worship itself is a political act. We declare allegiance, we pledge devotion, we bow, we offer praise, we participate in establishment rituals, and we bond as a community of common faith and practice. One of the issues in the churches was the intrusion of the empire narrative into the narrative of the slaughtered Lamb. The false teachers and deceivers were named and confronted in the letters. If the empire is able to infiltrate the Christian story, we are in essence being assimilated into a different story from the one we were saved into. This is a significant concern for the church today. We are mesmerized by entertainment, compromised by a quasi gospel of success, devoted to the trappings of imperial rewards, and avoiding the costly obedience that may bring suffering.

Worship in the Revelation is a simple choice: beast or Lamb? In embracing one, the other is diminished as ruler of our hearts. Dean Flemming writes,

> Christians in Asia Minor faced daily pressures to participate in Roman public life, which was entangled with the "civil religion" of the emperor cult and the worship of traditional gods. For John, however, compromising with the ways of the empire meant colluding with a whole system of imperial power—religious, economic and political. It placed them in league with a competing rule/empire, which claimed an allegiance that God alone deserved.
>
> John, then, has a dual purpose for Revelation. Negatively, he seeks to distance these communities from the empire's ways of thinking and living. Positively, he calls them to an unrivaled worship of the one sovereign God and to bear prophetic witness to God and his mission in the world.[1]

---

1. Dean Flemming, "Living Out the Future: Missional Ecclesiology in the Book of Revelation," *Didache: Faithful Teaching* 13, no. 2 (Winter 2014): 2, https://didache.nazarene.org/index.php/gtc2013/bible/902-revelation-bible-flemming-eng/file.

The worship of God is as much about a "deep no" as a "deep yes." The problem is that the worship of many is a "mixed maybe." They lack the confession of the Bad News about the false premise of the empire. They prefer to hold the prize of social position, economic prosperity, and civic esteem in one hand, while singing praise to the Lamb from the hymnal in the other. The dualistic nature of apocalyptic literature leaves little room for embracing both. Obedience in the Revelation comes down again to the simple choice of worshipping the beast or the Lamb.

> The worship of God is as much about a "deep no" as a "deep yes." The problem is that the worship of many is a "mixed maybe."

Michael Gorman suggests that "the imperial cult was an elaborate 'God and country' phenomenon, or type of 'civic' or civil religion, that in various ways attributed a sacred character to the Roman Empire and to the emperor himself."[2] He goes on to demonstrate how Rome manifests a religious character by doing the following: declaring that the gods have chosen Rome; suggesting that the rulers of Rome are the agents of the gods; naming blessing (security, peace, etc.) as the reward of the gods to those who submit to Roman rule; ensuring enforcement of the rule through domination; giving the emperor quasi-divine titles that made him worthy of prayers, praise, and sacrifices; and claiming that the imperial age was the eschatological golden age for human hopes.[3]

The pathway to devotion and worship runs through the desires of the heart. Rome understood this and incorporated sensual experiences

---

2. Gorman. *Reading Revelation Responsibly*, 41.
3. Ibid., 41-42.

in the coronations, guild worship, and public festivals. Rome understood the human desire to aspire to something greater and larger, and filled the gap with the religion of the empire. This is similar to our current worship-idolatry of materialism. Jamie Smith writes,

> I think we should first recognize and admit that the marketing industry—which promises an erotically charged transcendence through media that connects to our heart and imagination—is operating with a better, more creational, more incarnational, more holistic anthropology than much [of the Christian world]. In other words, I think we must admit that the marketing industry is able to capture, form, and direct our desires precisely because they have rightly discerned that we are embodied, desiring creatures whose being-in-the-world is governed by imagination. Marketers have figured out the way to our heart because they "get it": they rightly understand that, at root, we are *erotic* creatures—creatures who are oriented primarily by love and passion and desire. In sum, I think Victoria is in on [a] secret.[4]

If Smith is right about human desiring, and I believe he is, then it is essential that Christian worship engage the senses of the human as a path to the desires. This cannot be done with doctrinal formulations and religious lectures alone. We do not think our way to a different way of living. We imagine and then live our way to a different way of thinking. John is offering a new imagination to the seven churches, a different experience, a new story in which to see themselves living. The practices of the holy life ground us in the theology of the holy life.

---

4. James K. A. Smith, *Desiring the Kingdom: Worship, Worldview, and Cultural Formation* (Grand Rapids: Baker Academic, 2009), 75-76.

We already *know* more than we *do*. Our failure is not in knowing but in practicing the way of Jesus. And when the essence of Christianity is boiled down to its base, we are called to be disciples, followers of the Lamb. Then we are taught the doctrinal foundation for the way of life that we have been invited to follow. Those who offer corporate worship to the people of God must engage the senses along with the mind.

The act of worship in the Revelation is as sensual as any that we find in the Bible. All the senses are engaged. We are constantly told to "see," "look," and "behold." Our eyes attend a parade of sights, colors, shapes, explosions, brightness, darkness, huge numbers, diverse peoples, hideous beasts, animals, and images. Our ears hear the sound of mighty waters, the cry of saints beneath the altars, the announcements of angels, the singing of living creatures, and the sound of the multitudes.

> **The Revelation is not a boring lecture that our droopy eyes and tired ears endure. It is a pyrotechnic, sensual display of the grand story of the universe.**

Our noses smell acrid sulfur, smoke, the sweetness of fruit, the burning of human flesh, the stench of a decaying city, and the incense at the throne. Our sense of touch receives the impression of pounding waves, a trembling earth, a scroll placed in our hands, and the heat of the sun. Our tongue tastes bloody water, a sweet and bitter scroll, the gift of the water of life, and the fruit of the trees that heal the nations.

The Revelation is not a boring lecture that our droopy eyes and tired ears endure. It is a pyrotechnic, sensual display of the grand story of the universe. It is thunderously loud and breath-stoppingly quiet, stunningly bright and frighteningly dark, calmingly peaceful and alarmingly chaotic. From one tornadic drop down to the next, we are on the edge of our seats. The worship of the Revelation engages bodies because it addresses every aspect of who we are.

The practice of Christian worship includes honest confession of the beastly counterfeit, but there is also the lament of the saints. Too often in our gatherings, we play nice with God rather than ask our painful questions. The people who can gust at seventy miles per hour condemning the evil of the empire quite often do not know how to petition God for justice. I have been in services that focus only on the Bad News. The people and preacher spend all their emotive energy attacking the evil beyond the walls of the church. I find that this is often a diversion from hearing the Good News and discovering the obedience called for in it. If the congregation is only centered on complaint, the result on the street will be minimal. The corrective for this is lament. We learn this in the Old Testament psalms where the people of God ask for justice.

We rarely read the lament psalms-prayers in church. They are an expression of raw human emotion in response to things that make no sense: enemies who get away with evil, senseless murder, the absence of God. But these prayers made the editor's cut and have become the prayers of the people of God. Although they may not be useful for mundane days, they are ours to pray when darkness seems to hide God's face. Sometimes God is inexplicable. The cry of lament from the martyrs punctuates the Revelation:

> When he opened the fifth seal, I saw under the altar the souls of those who had been slaughtered for the word of God and for the testimony they had given; they cried out with a loud voice, "Sovereign Lord, holy and true, how long will it be before you judge and avenge our blood on the inhabitants of the earth?" They were each given a white robe and told to rest a little longer, until the number would be complete both of their fellow servants and of their brothers and sisters, who were soon to be killed as they themselves had been killed. (6:9-11)

These prayers are haunting. They confess what we all wonder: If God is sovereign and good, why do God's people suffer and die under the beastly powers? Many consider such questioning to be a lack of faith. But the scriptural practice of crying out in lament is both welcomed by God and is actually an act of faith. We believe that God is just and that it is in God's nature to bring justice to the earth. We are taught this in the Lord's Prayer as we pray for the will of God to be done on earth, even as it is done in heaven, and for the kingdom of God to come to earth. Jesus is the beginning of this right-making divine work, and Jesus is the agent of all things being made new.

Worship as a response of the people of God includes the antiworship of the beast, the true worship of the Lamb, honest confession about the deathly ways of the empire, expressed allegiance, desiring hearts, a biblical lament for justice, and the deep hope that God will restore all creation.

Testimony as a Response of the People

From my childhood, I have enjoyed the gatherings for worship in which people stood to testify to the work of God in their lives. These testimonies were deeply personal, often a mininarrative of saving grace or a specific thanksgiving for divine intervention. No book in Scripture mentions testimony more often than the Revelation.

Two terms of similar origin are used interchangeably—"witness" and "testimony." Both find their home in a court of law. Those seeking to determine guilt and innocence seek true witnesses. In a sense, this is in keeping with the throne of God being situated at the center of the Revelation. God's throne in the Old Testament was often viewed as the site of a heavenly hearing. In the Revelation, we find testimony mentioned often in relation to the activity around the throne. Even Satan testifies in accusation against the saints. The word "witness" also denotes a martyr, a person killed by political powers due to the words they speak. Christians on trial for their faith were often threatened with execution unless they were willing to recant their faith in God and declare that Caesar is Lord. Witnessing could be a costly act that could lead to martyrdom.

Jesus is, first and foremost, "the faithful witness" of the Revelation (1:5). In the letter to Laodicea, Jesus is "the Amen, the faithful and true witness" (2:14). As the rider on the white horse in 19:11-16, his single weapon is the sword that comes from his mouth and his victory over the evil trinity is secured by his words. Several times it is noted that his judgments are trustworthy and true. Revelation 22:16 closes the book with the reiteration that Jesus is the one whose angel brings this testimony to the churches.

"Prophecy" is another word that refers to a faithful message. In the opening and closing of the book, the visions are called prophecy.[5] A prophet is the mouthpiece of God, a divinely anointed messenger. Jesus is both faithful witness and prophet of truth.

John is also referred to as a faithful witness. In the opening verses, John testifies "to the word of God and to the testimony of Jesus Christ, even to all that he saw" (1:2). John sees the exalted Son of Man and is told to write down what he sees and deliver it to the churches (vv. 19-20). He is an entrusted messenger. In the final chapter, he is made the caretaker of the message lest anyone add to or subtract from what is written in the scrolls. John is a faithful witness and a prophet of God.

At Pergamum we meet the one named martyr in the Revelation—Antipas. The letter states, "I know where you are living, where Satan's throne is. Yet you are holding fast to my name, and you did not deny your faith in me even in the days of Antipas my witness, my faithful one, who was killed among you, where Satan lives" (2:13). More than likely, the empire offered to spare his life if he would recant his faith in God, but he refused.

Around the time of the Revelation, the leader of the church in Smyrna was a faithful man named Polycarp. At age eighty-six, he was tried, condemned, and burned alive. The Roman ruler gave Polycarp an out by suggesting that he revile Christ and offer sacrifice to Caesar. Polycarp replied, "For eighty-six years I have been his slave, and he has

---

5. See ch. 1, "The Revelation: Apocalypse, Prophecy, and Epistle," for the accounting of prophetic literature in the Revelation.

done me no wrong. How can I blaspheme my King who saved me?"[6] On hearing this, the hostile crowd erupted in anger. They gathered wood for the burning, and afterward prohibited the Christians from taking Polycarp's body for burial. Disciples like Antipas and Polycarp had defined the meaning of martyrdom. Their uncompromising testimony of the Lamb was a reflection of the life of Jesus.

The call of the Revelation to Christians was to bear faithful witness. We see the two witnesses in Revelation 11. They bear testimony (prophesy) in the streets of the great city until they are killed by the beast. After three and a half days, God raises them as a vindication of their witness. In Revelation 12, we find the saints who participate with the archangel Michael in the eviction of Satan from heaven. They defeated the dragon by the blood of the Lamb and the word of their testimony. Throughout the Apocalypse, we see believers bearing testimony to the Lamb. The 144,000 who are sealed with the mark of God reflect a faithful following of the Lamb in testimony. The saints we meet at the throne and in the scenes of conquest are distinguished by their faithful witness. Churches are also referred to as lampstands (1:20; 2:1). The people of God are called to respond to the cosmic victory by shining the light of this good news in the dark streets of the great city. While they are not the light, they are bearers of the light.

It is important that we not truncate this response of the people by limiting it to spoken words. Jesus is the faithful witness, not just by the words he speaks, but by the cruciform life he lives. His suffering love is a testimony. Doing the Father's will, serving the outcasts, identifying

---

6. *The Martyrdom of Polycarp*, in *The Apostolic Fathers*, trans. J. B. Lightfoot and J. R. Harmer, 2nd ed., ed. Michael W. Holmes (Grand Rapids: Baker Book House, 1989), 139.

with the excluded, taking up a cross, and laying down his life are all part and parcel of a faithful witness. The faithful are those who "did not cling to life even in the face of death" (12:11).

Flemming writes,

What, then, are God's missional people to *do*? Above all, their role is to bear faithful *witness*. In the first place, this means giving verbal testimony (*martyria*) to the word and truth of God . . . , empowered by the prophetic Spirit (19:10). But the church does not bear witness with words alone. Its testimony is anchored in "Jesus Christ, the faithful witness" (1:5), and Jesus' unswerving witness led him to the cross. To follow the slain Lamb, likewise, means to bear witness and suffer. . . . Through their suffering witness of word and life, they also share in the Lamb's triumph.⁷

The tendency of Christians to exalt words over deeds, doctrine over practice, verbal testimony over sacrificial suffering, is visible today. It is not uncommon to see someone attacking another over an issue of doctrine, and the meanness of their spirit speaks louder than the truth of their critique. The pursuit of right doctrine seems to justify any violation of love. I am not suggesting that right theological thought is unimportant. It is our responsibility to love the Lord with all our mind and to be formed by the mind of Christ. But if our faithful witness is only in the head, we have missed the mark of what it means to be disciples of the Lamb.

> **If our faithful witness is only in the head, we have missed the mark of what it means to be disciples of the Lamb.**

---

7. Flemming, "Living out the Future," 3.

In *The Universal Christ*, Richard Rohr comments on witness that is co-opted by the empire.

Is our only mission to merely keep announcing our vision and philosophy statement? Sometimes it has seemed that way. This is what happens when power and empire take over the message.

Did you know that the first seven Councils of the Church, agreed upon by both East and West, were all either convened or formally presided over by emperors? This is no small point. Emperors and governments do not tend to be interested in an ethic of love, service, or nonviolence (God forbid!), and surely not forgiveness unless it somehow helps them stay in power.

. . . Mere information is rarely helpful unless it also enlightens and "amorizes" [kindles love in] your life. . . . Any good idea that does not engage the body, the heart, the physical world, and the people around us will tend to be more theological problem solving and theory than any real healing of people and institutions—which ironically is about all Jesus does!

. . . You wouldn't guess this from the official creeds but, after all is said and done, doing is more important than saying. Jesus was clearly more concerned with . . . "right action" ("orthopraxy" in Christianity) than with right saying, or even right thinking. You can hear this message very clearly in his parable of the two sons in Matthew 21:28-31: One son says he won't work in the vineyard, but then does, while the other says he will go, but in fact doesn't. Jesus told his listeners that he preferred the one who actually goes, although saying the wrong words, over the one who says the right words but does not act. How did we miss that?[8]

One other significant response of witness is the work of vocation. It is easy to read the Revelation with the thought that God opposes economic work, artisan skills, the making of money, and the gatherings of guilds and unions. The cult of the emperor has so intertwined its region with the economic world of Rome that we have a hard time imagining a Christian theology of work in the Revelation. The one note that redeems this is found in the description of the new Jerusalem. In 21:24, we see the nations of the earth walking by the light of the Lamb and "the kings of the earth" bringing "their glory into" the city. This glory can be understood as art, skill, merchandise, music, learning—every human thriving that occurred under the rule of kings. It is welcomed into the city as an act of worship laid at the feet of the Lamb.

Although vocation is not a dominant theme in the Revelation, we must not interpret the Revelation as an escape from the economic world. Christians are called to labor, to provide for their families and those in need, and to serve their fellow humans by the work of their hands. Discerning where the Roman economy ends as worship of the beast and where fulfilling our God-given vocation begins as an expression of worship will always be a challenge for the disciples of Jesus. We cannot worship God and mammon, Lamb and beast, but we do live in a world of work, currency, and economic power. This dilemma is not always easy.

---

8. Richard Rohr, *The Universal Christ: How a Forgotten Reality Can Change Everything We See, Hope for, and Believe* (New York: Convergent Books, 2019), 104-6.

Social Justice as a Response of the People

Some have suggested that the narrative of the Revelation views the people of God as resisting but not opposing the empire. The victory gained over the evil trinity has the white-robed saints on their horses, but they do nothing. The sword in the mouth of the Lamb wins the victory. The directives to the chided churches never call on them to confront the empire. The actions suggested are doable within the context of the congregation but rarely spill over into a public stance. The people of God are waiting, praying for justice, resisting participation, and bearing faithful witness without compromise, but they do not take a public stance in their cities. Are we to conclude from this that we should not confront the powers that run the dark empires of our world? I think not.

The context of powerlessness often suggests what is possible and what is not. There are settings in which a quiet, careful witness is the wisest strategy for fulfilling the mission of God. Many of our missionaries, in assignments where Christians are forbidden to be, can help us understand how the gospel goes forth in such a challenged setting. But most of us do not live in this context. We have the capacity and responsibility to testify in the public square. We can imagine the kingdom of God out loud. We can enact it in what we endorse and what we oppose.

One of the ways that the Revelation imagines a world made new is in the multinational community that is celebrated. Every time we see the saints of God, they are from every nation, language, and tribe. This means that the people of the seven churches were to extend their fellowship to the disempowered of their day. Roman citizenship was needed for most of the empire's privileges. The church was called to welcome all, to stand with the disenfranchised, to include the excluded. This is the beginning of biblical social justice, which runs counter to the world's values. Rome takes care of Romans at the expense of everyone else. The church sacrifices itself to care for the outsider. The early church distinguished itself in the empire by the way it cared for orphan and widow, foreigner and stranger, great and small, free and slave. The diversity imagined at the throne of God led believers to see the current church as a gathering of all peoples under allegiance to the Lamb.

I write this on the day after the Martin Luther King Jr. national holiday. The most powerful letter I have ever read is his "Letter from Birmingham Jail." It humbles me every time I read it. While the Revelation never instructs the saints in nonviolent protest, marches, or peaceful resistance, I cannot help but hear echoes of the imagined new Jerusalem in the speeches and dreams of Martin Luther King Jr. The Revelation inspires resistance and opposition to the evil that diminishes the inhabitants of the earth. Yet we know that it is not our action but the power of the Lamb that ultimately conquers evil. Social justice as a response of the people of God requires a full confidence in the God who comes to rule, even as it inspires our faithful resistance to the evil that rules where we currently live.

Borrowing from the letter of James,

You must understand this, my beloved: let everyone be quick to listen, slow to speak, slow to anger; for your anger does not produce

God's righteousness. Therefore rid yourselves of all sordidness and rank growth of wickedness, and welcome with meekness the implanted word that has the power to save your souls.

But be doers of the word, and not merely hearers who deceive themselves. For if any are hearers of the word and not doers, they are like those who look at themselves in a mirror; for they look at themselves and, on going away, immediately forget what they were like. But those who look into the perfect law, the law of liberty, and persevere, being not hearers who forget but doers who act—they will be blessed in their doing.

If any think they are religious, and do not bridle their tongues but deceive their hearts, their religion is worthless. Religion that is pure and undefiled before God, the Father, is this: to care for orphans and widows in their distress, and to keep oneself unstained by the world. (1:19-27)

In a similar way, the Revelation is a blessing to those who read "aloud the words of the prophecy" and "those who hear and *who keep what is written in it*" (1:3, emphasis added). The saints are expected to respond to the Good News as obedient children. In the Revelation, this most often takes the form of worship, testimony, vocational witness, and social justice.

Prayer

Gracious God, your saving deeds motivate us to action.
All that you have done inspires all that we might do.
You have sent your Holy Spirit to enlighten our
minds that we may know what you desire.
And your Spirit dreams within our imaginations
what our obedience looks like.
The power to act is a gracious gift from you.
It is not by our strength but by your Spirit that we overcome.
May our worship, our witness, our work, and our deeds of justice
reflect the ministry of your Son, Jesus.
Amen.

6

Blessing-Benediction

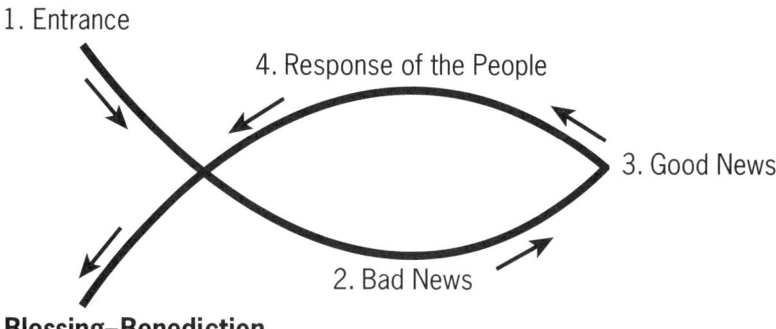

We come to the final act in the plot of worship. It is the blessing-benediction, which sends the people of God into the world. In Scripture, a blessing is words invested with the power to do good. A curse is words invested with the power to harm. The world curses us. The world curses the Lamb that we worship because his victory limits and constrains evil. The world steals, kills, and destroys. The world's lies seduce us to sleep with the prostitute empire. God's blessing counters the curse.

Many call the closing prayer of worship the "benediction." This term means "good words" (*bene* [good] + *diction* [words]). In a Bad News world, we are sent out under the blessing of good words spoken over us.

"You wanna know why I come to church?" she asked me.

"Sure," I replied.

"I come for the blessing. When you raise your hands at the end of the service and say those good words, well . . . it's the only time something like that happens to me during the week. Everywhere else I get dumped on. When you bless us, I feel like I can live another week."

I'll never forget that conversation. The young woman was right. *Blessing* is essential to life in the streets of the great city where the prostitute prowls. We send the people of God into the world under the blessing of God. We depart to serve under the smile and favor of God. We are invigorated by the Spirit of God. We are going out where Jesus goes. We are children of the Father. The Trinity is at work in us.

Blessing is empowering. It reminds people that God is at work in their Response and will be at work in their world. It gives boldness to beaten down people. It whispers gracious words to those who hear grumbling all week long. It invades damaged esteem with Creator value. And it counters the curse of the world.

> **Blessing is empowering. It reminds people that God is at work in their Response and will be at work in their world.**

Most of the New Testament letters end with blessing. Hebrews concludes by saying, "Now may the God of peace, who brought back from the dead our Lord Jesus, the great shepherd of the sheep, by the blood of the eternal covenant, make you complete in everything good so that you may do his will, working among us that which is pleasing in his sight, through Jesus Christ, to whom be the glory forever and ever. Amen" (13:20-21). Philippians ends, "The grace of the Lord Jesus Christ be with your spirit" (Phil. 4:23). Paul's second letter to Corinth concludes with, "The grace of the Lord Jesus Christ, the love of God, and the communion of the Holy Spirit be with all of you" (13:13).

The Revelation has blessings scattered throughout, and it ends with a benediction. As you might guess, there are seven blessings. They stretch from the opening verses to the closing verses.

- "Blessed is the one who reads aloud the words of the prophecy, and blessed are those who hear and who keep what is written in it; for the time is near" (1:3).
- "And I heard a voice from heaven saying, 'Write this: Blessed are the dead who from now on die in the Lord.' 'Yes,' says the Spirit, 'they will rest from their labors, for their deeds will follow them'" (14:13).
- "See, I am coming like a thief! Blessed is the one who stays awake and is clothed, not going about naked and exposed to shame" (16:15).
- "And the angel said to me, 'Write this: Blessed are those who are invited to the marriage supper of the Lamb.' And he said to me, 'These are the true words of God'" (19:9).
- "Blessed and holy are those who share in the first resurrection. Over these the second death has no power, but they will be priests of God and of Christ, and they will reign with him a thousand years" (20:6).
- "See, I am coming soon! Blessed is the one who keeps the words of the prophecy of this book" (22:7).

- "Blessed are those who wash their robes, so that they will have the right to the tree of life and may enter the city by the gates" (22:14).

God is laying claim to the obedient, to the watchful, to those fully clothed in righteousness, and to all who are invited to the supper of the Lamb. God is speaking good words over those who have been martyred and who are raised to reign with Christ. If you look at each beatitude, you see that the saints resemble the Son—obedient to God, clothed in righteous deeds, sufferers for their faith, crucified, raised to reign, and destined for the marriage supper of the Lamb.

The five moves of the worship story have internal connections. Moves one and five are paired—Entrance and Blessing. We enter the presence of God and the Lamb and are located in an event that restores us in the likeness of this God. We exit corporate worship under divine blessing, sent out in resemblance of the Lamb. Our allegiance and devotion are to the ways of the Lamb.

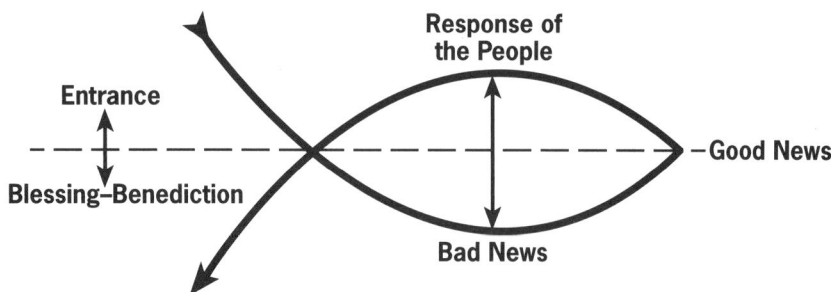

Moves two and four are also paired—Bad News and Response of the People. The inhabitants of the earth, including those gathered in worship, have behaved badly—idolatry, compromise, assimilation, and complacency. But we are changed in the act of worship to behave differently. Our Response is the exact opposite of the Bad News. Where we were idolaters, we have become God worshippers. Where we were pawns of Satan, we have become the priests of God. Where we were dead, we have been made alive. Where we were compromised, we have been consecrated.

The hinge in the middle of the five moves is the Good News. This makes all the difference. The activity of God on our behalf is the redeeming pivot for all of creation. When we enter the presence of God, confess our distance from and opposition to this God, we are met with the Good News that reconciles and redeems us. This makes us capable of a faithful Response of the People, which marks us as the Blessed and sent-out children of God.

I have suggested that the Revelation is plotted something like a tornado that spirals in place with great force and then lifts from the ground until it sets down again. Is it possible that our lives follow the same pattern? Once every seven days, we gather around the story of God in common worship. We Enter God's presence; we confess the Bad News of the world we participate in and are tempted by; we proclaim the Good News of the activity of God; we then Respond in worship, testimony, vocation, and social justice; and we are sent back into the world under divine Blessing. We have stepped into a powerful tornado that rearranges our understanding of the world. Everything that the world had securely nailed down is spun in the air by the vision of the coming kingdom. Every lofty claim of the empire is blown away.

Every established power is uprooted from its throne. Worship takes on empire and unsettles it and us and then sends us for six days of normal, but with a new imagination. Then on the seventh day, we repeat our act of worship, and the world is reinterpreted from the perspective of the Lamb, and we are sent again into the world to live according to the vision that is shaping us.

I can only imagine what the week following the reading of the Revelation was like in the cities of the seven churches. And lest we limit the message to them, the fact that there were seven churches is God's way of saying the whole church, all the churches, all the people of God. These letters have our addresses, and the Spirit is speaking to us today. We live among empires that call for our worship. We exist where beasts roam looking to mark us. We are tempted to complacency and compromise in the face of costly obedience. We are faced daily with the primary question of the Revelation: beast or Lamb?

Prayer

Gracious God, may we hear what the Spirit says
to the church through the Revelation.
And may our hearing become doing until the world recognizes us
as people who live under divine favor and calling.
May our mission be your mission.
Strengthen our resolve to live according to the mark of the Lamb.
Amen.

Bibliography

Baring-Gould, Sabine. "Onward, Christian Soldiers." In *Sing to the Lord*. Kansas City: Lillenas Publishing Company, 1993, no. 644.

The Book of Common Prayer. New York: Seabury Press, 1979.

Boone, Dan. *Answers for Chicken Little*. Kansas City: Beacon Hill Press of Kansas City, 2005.

———. *The Worship Plot: Finding Unity in Our Common Story*. Kansas City: Beacon Hill Press of Kansas City, 2007.

Boring, M. Eugene. *Revelation*. Interpretation: A Bible Commentary for Teaching and Preaching. Louisville, KY: John Knox Press, 1989.

Brueggemann, Walter. "Counterscript: Living with the Elusive God." *Christian Century*, November 29, 2005, 22-28.

Daniels, T. Scott. *Seven Deadly Spirits: The Message of Revelation's Letters for Today's Church*. Grand Rapids: Baker Academic, 2009.

Flemming, Dean. "Living Out the Future: Missional Ecclesiology in the Book of Revelation," *Didache: Faithful Teaching* 13, no. 2 (Winter 2014): 2, https://didache.nazarene.org/index.php/gtc2013/bible/902-revelation-bible-flemming-eng/file.

Gorman, Michael J. *Reading Revelation Responsibly: Uncivil Worship and Witness: Following the Lamb into the New Creation*. Eugene, OR: Cascade Books, 2011.

Harder, Cherie. Introduction to *Selections from a Brave New World*. Trinity Forum Readings (Trinity Forum, 2018), https://www.ttf.org/product/brave-new-world/.

Heber, Reginald. "Holy, Holy, Holy! Lord God Almighty." In *Sing to the Lord*. Kansas City: Lillenas Publishing Company, 1993, no. 2.

Koester, Craig R. *Revelation and the End of All Things*. Grand Rapids: Eerdmans, 2001.

The Martyrdom of Polycarp. In *The Apostolic Fathers*, translated by J. B. Lightfoot and J. R. Harmer. 2nd ed., edited by Michael W. Holmes. Grand Rapids: Baker Book House, 1989.

Moltmann, Jürgen. *The Coming of God: Christian Eschatology*. Translated by Margaret Kohl. Minneapolis: Fortress Press, 1996.

Peterson, Eugene. *Reversed Thunder: The Revelation of John and the Praying Imagination*. San Francisco: HarperSanFrancisco, 1991.

———. *Working the Angles: The Shape of Pastoral Integrity*. Grand Rapids: Eerdmans, 1987.

Rohr, Richard. *The Universal Christ: How a Forgotten Reality Can Change Everything We See, Hope for, and Believe*. New York: Convergent Books, 2019.

Smith, James K. A. *Desiring the Kingdom: Worship, Worldview, and Cultural Formation*. Grand Rapids: Baker Academic, 2009.

Taylor, Barbara Brown. "Preaching the Terrors." *Leadership Journal* (Spring 1992): 45.

Truesdale, Al. "The Genre of the Book of Revelation." A Resource for Clergy of the Tennessee District Church of the Nazarene. 2013 Seminar.

Wright, N. T. *Revelation for Everyone*. Louisville, KY: Westminster John Knox Press, 2011.